THE **ESSENTIAL** GUIDE TO BORDEAUX WINES

THE ESSENTIAL GUIDE TO BORDEAUX WINES

IN COLLABORATION WITH THE BORDEAUX WINE SCHOOL

Written with the help of Sophie Brissaud

STEWART, TABORI & CHANG
NEW YORK

Table of contents

What is the meaning of the name 'Bordeaux' in today's wine world? In a time when wine, like everything else, is following the way of globalization, when the identity of a region or a terroir is affected by a global move towards standardization of taste, what is the magic formula that gives Bordeaux wines their timeless appeal? The answer to these questions is not to be sought in the ponderous heritage of a time-honored status, but in something more intimate and secret that hides in the heart of a glass of Bordeaux wine, far beyond its physical, chemical and mineral components. That secret, intimate element may be described as equilibrium – a balance experienced through the many colors of Bordeaux wines: red, white, pink, the coral of a clairet, the gold of a sweet wine, the pale blond foam of a crémant. Not to mention the infinite variations produced by blending. This balance may be experienced as you lean closer to the earth: you may feel it in the energy rising from the soil, in a mosaic of unique terroirs, where wine growing and winemaking have retained their artisan character, the result of traditional skills perfected by the most recent scientific discoveries on the biology of the vine plant and the properties of soils, and of an ever-increasing concern for nature and the environment.

In that glass, you may hear the distant echo of the work of winemakers who, one generation after another, patiently crafted these liquid works of art from the precious matter gifted by nature. Between their hands, merlots, cabernets, sauvignons, sémillons are like keys on a keyboard or colors on a palette – indeed the art of blending was invented in Bordeaux, and it is through that art that grape varieties, through that sublime synergy, produce ever more complex and amazing wines.

A wonderful bouquet of complex qualities lies in a glass of Bordeaux. This book aims to help you understand their secrets, which you may share with others in turn. In Bordeaux, the capital city of wine culture, your initiation to equilibrium is now beginning.

1

THE WINES OF BORDEAUX,
AN OVERVIEW

BORDEAUX AND THE WORLD

The wine region of Bordeaux is a gift of nature, born at the confluence of two major rivers, between earth and sea. For two thousand years, its history has been so intricately connected with the city of the same name that the two are almost indistinguishable, the vineyard having shaped the entire region in a deep and thorough manner. A quick overview of the current situation of the Bordeaux region in a global context reveals its unique character and may help explain why, to a large number of people, the name of Bordeaux simply means wine.

LET'S TRAVEL THROUGH TIME...

The origin of winemaking can be located in the Near East, in an area that covers Georgia, Armenia and north Iran. One has to wait until about 2,500 years BC to find the first written or archeological traces of cultivated vine in Mesopotamia. In the 6th century BC, Greek and Phenician navigators introduced the grape vine in Gaul through the port of Marseilles. Later, in the 1st century BC, the Romans established a vast vineyard in Gallia Narbonensis, a region founded around the city of Narbonne. However, for a long period of time, the grape varieties they were using prospered only in warm climates, making the extension of vine-growing to the north impossible beyond a certain limit (the current location of Gaillac, in Southwestern France, and L'Hermitage, in the Rhône valley). During that era, wine growing was almost exclusively a Mediterranean affair.

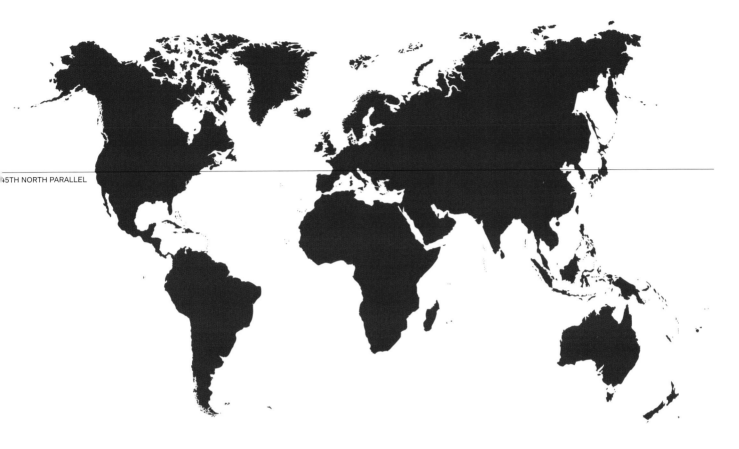

45TH NORTH PARALLEL

THAT 45TH NORTH PARALLEL

According to a famous theory, the 45th north Parallel — which runs exactly through the Bordeaux region — is the perfect line of latitude for making the greatest wines in the world; it is also a limit on either side of which winemaking answers to different rules: south of that line, the conditions are supposedly better for red wines, while north of that line they seem more adapted to white wines. Therefore the perfect vine-growing zone lies between the 40th and 50th parallels.

The situation changed drastically around the 1st century AD: the Celtic tribe of the Bituriges Vivisques founded the city of Burdigala, now Bordeaux. A former warring tribe, they embraced a life of trading and agriculture, thus laying the bases of a particular glamorous lifestyle that still characterizes the region, which is naturally endowed with a mild climate and a fertile soil, at the confluence of two major rivers — the Garonne and the Dordogne. In the 4th century AD, Bordelais poet Ausonius (309-394) passionately celebrated the excellent local fare in his verse, not forgetting to mention the wines. In fact, the Bituriges Vivisques had the excellent idea of introducing a new grape variety in the region: biturica, a stock that proved more resistant to the cold weather than the Southern varieties that had been hitherto grown in the southern half of Gaul. This grape biturica happens to be the ancestor of our modern cabernets…

The innovative introduction of biturica opened new horizons and started the true era of Bordeaux winemaking — not only in Bordeaux, but in Europe, and later in other parts of the world.

BORDEAUX IN THE 21ST CENTURY:
THE LARGEST AOC (PDO) VINEYARD IN FRANCE

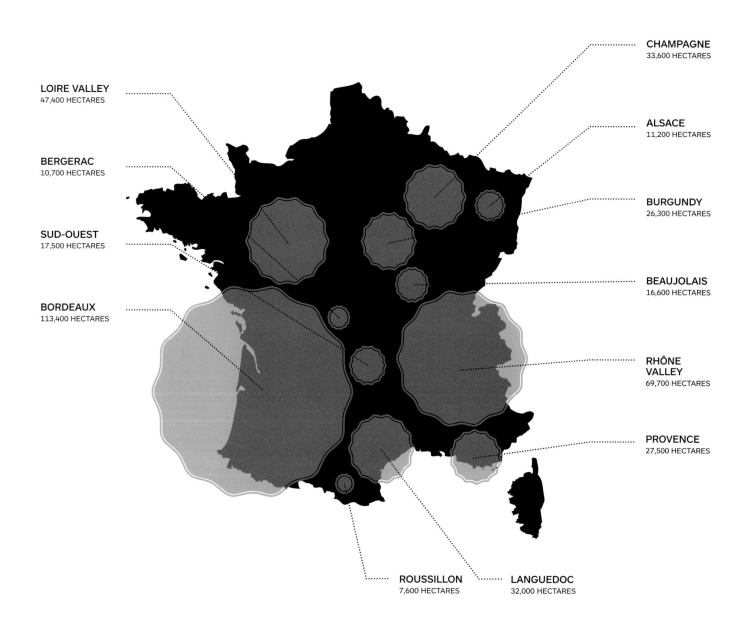

CHAMPAGNE
33,600 HECTARES

LOIRE VALLEY
47,400 HECTARES

ALSACE
11,200 HECTARES

BERGERAC
10,700 HECTARES

BURGUNDY
26,300 HECTARES

SUD-OUEST
17,500 HECTARES

BEAUJOLAIS
16,600 HECTARES

BORDEAUX
113,400 HECTARES

RHÔNE
VALLEY
69,700 HECTARES

PROVENCE
27,500 HECTARES

ROUSSILLON
7,600 HECTARES

LANGUEDOC
32,000 HECTARES

CIVB, SOURCE: THE INTERPROFESSION, 2013 DATA.

THE REFERENCE VINEYARD

Many people see Bordeaux wines as the archetype of wine, with good reason: throughout history, many innovations in the region have marked the history of winemaking. Here are a few:

— The introduction of weather-resistant grape varieties has allowed wine growers to extend their activity to cooler regions.

— In the 17th century, in the Graves region, "modern" red wines with long-keeping qualities, such as we know them today, were invented.

— Bordeaux also invented blending, which allowed wine-makers to build wonderfully balanced wines by combining the best qualities of each variety.

— The adoption of the glass bottle allowed to carry and keep wines in a new manner (the first glass factory that specialized in wine bottles was created in Bordeaux by Pierre Mitchell, in 1723).

— The invention of the concept of a wine château paved the way for the notion of wine estate, and of the distinctive wines produced thereon and being given a related name.

— Bordeaux is constantly on the front line of technological progress and diffusion of oenological knowledge, as shown through teaching programs and world-famous research centers (such as the Université de la vigne et du vin — or ISVV, the Institute of Vine and Wine Sciences).

In many respects, Bordeaux played an important part in the shaping of modern wine-growing and winemaking, and remains today the world's reference vineyard.

BORDEAUX IN THE WORLD: A FEW FIGURES

What is Bordeaux's position in the world wine market?

In 2013, the world production of wine amounted to nearly 277 million hectoliters, produced on a surface of slightly less than 7.5 million hectares of vineyards. The European continent remains the largest production zone, including 56% of total world surface. France, Italy and Spain are the top producing countries. Together, they represent 47% of the world's total wine production. Bordeaux, with its 113,000 hectares of AOC (PDO) vineyards, is the first wine region in France for Protected Designation of Origin. The amount of wine produced in Bordeaux represents 15% of France's total production and 1.5% of world production.

France, which is among the top world countries for wine consumption (about 48 liters per person and per year), is the primary outlet for Bordeaux wines, concentrating 58% of the commercialized volumes.

THE APPELLATIONS OF THE BORDEAUX WINE REGION (IN HECTARES)

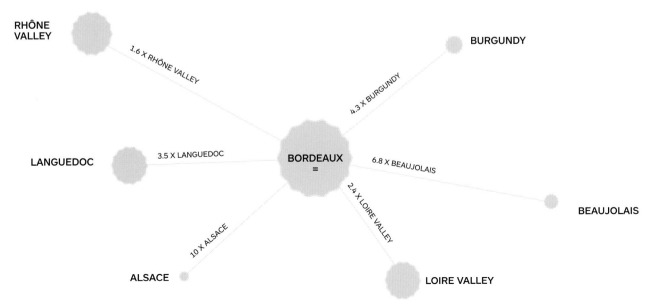

RHÔNE VALLEY — 1.6 X RHÔNE VALLEY

BURGUNDY — 4.3 X BURGUNDY

LANGUEDOC — 3.5 X LANGUEDOC

BORDEAUX =

6.8 X BEAUJOLAIS — BEAUJOLAIS

2.4 X LOIRE VALLEY — LOIRE VALLEY

10 X ALSACE — ALSACE

EXPORTING BORDEAUX

Since Medieval times, Bordeaux always exported its wines. Where is it standing now?

Bordeaux wines represent about one fifth of the total amount of wines and spirits exported from France. They are the most significant export item of the Aquitaine region, ahead of aircraft manufacturing, with 17% of the export value. With an excess of 2.1 billion euros, the wine trade is the first exporter with a positive balance in the regional system.

Bordeaux wine exports split into three main geographical areas: East Asia — now massively dominated by China, which has been the number one destination in volume for Bordeaux since 2011; North America, and, in accordance with an age-old tradition, northern Europe (Germany, the UK, Belgium and Holland).

Regarding volume, the largest world importers of Bordeaux wines in 2013 were, in decreasing order: China, Germany, the UK, Belgium, Japan, the United States, Hong Kong, Canada, Holland, Switzerland, Lithuania, Cameroon, South Korea, Latvia and Poland.

When looking at value, the classification is different: the UK takes the first place, followed by China, then by Hong Kong, the United States, Germany, Switzerland, Belgium, Japan, Canada, Holland, Singapore, Taiwan, Macao, the United Arab Emirates, and Denmark.

In 2013, exports represented a little more than 40% of the commercialized volume of Bordeaux wines, which included slightly more than 2/5 to the European Union and about 3/5 to other countries and major export markets. The AOC Bordeaux and AOC Bordeaux Supérieur appellations make up the largest part of exported wines (60%), followed by Médoc and Graves (15%), dry whites (10%), Saint-Émilion-Pomerol-Fronsac (8%), Côtes (5%) and sweet whites (1%).

Since the early 2000s, in most cases, and particularly in times of crisis, the overseas trade has supported the entire region through exports, either limiting their fall or boosting their growth. The continuous growth of sales in recent years should be credited to the success of Bordeaux wines in the East Asian regions, particularly in China, as well as in North America.

SALES OF BORDEAUX WINES IN 2012 AND 2013, IN FRANCE AND ABROAD

23 BOTTLES OF BORDEAUX WINE ARE SOLD IN THE WORLD EVERY SECOND. IN 2012-2013, THE COMMERCIALIZATION OF BORDEAUX WINES REACHED 5.57 MILLION HECTOLITERS, THUS 743 MILLION BOTTLES, FOR A VALUE OF MORE THAN 4.2 BILLION EUROS.

DISTRIBUTION OF MARKETED VOLUMES

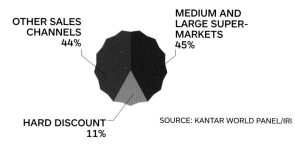

OTHER SALES CHANNELS 44%

MEDIUM AND LARGE SUPER-MARKETS 45%

HARD DISCOUNT 11%

SOURCE: KANTAR WORLD PANEL/IRI

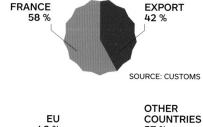

FRANCE 58 %

EXPORT 42 %

SOURCE: CUSTOMS

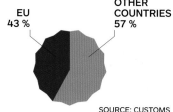

EU 43 %

OTHER COUNTRIES 57 %

SOURCE: CUSTOMS

TOP 15 DESTINATIONS FOR BORDEAUX WINES IN 2013

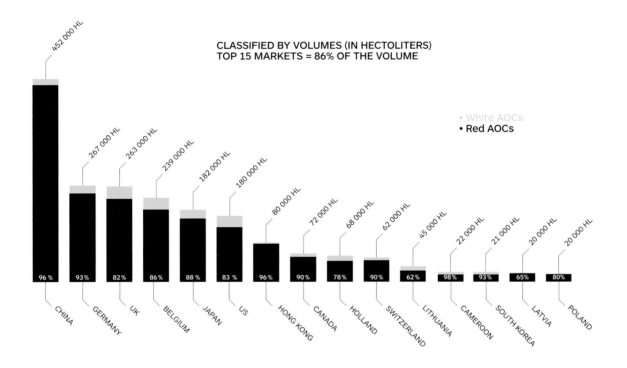

CLASSIFIED BY VOLUMES (IN HECTOLITERS)
TOP 15 MARKETS = 86% OF THE VOLUME

• White AOCs
• Red AOCs

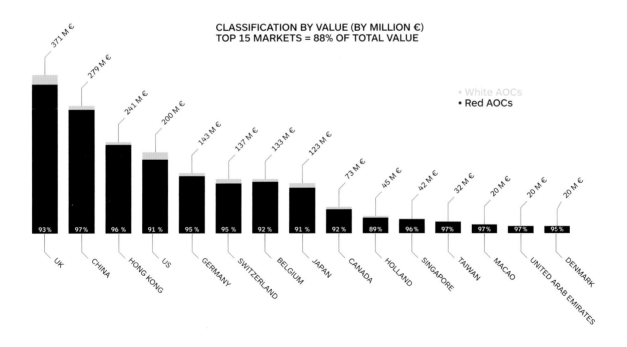

CLASSIFICATION BY VALUE (BY MILLION €)
TOP 15 MARKETS = 88% OF TOTAL VALUE

• White AOCs
• Red AOCs

CIVB - ECONOMY & RESEARCH / SOURCE: CUSTOMS

WHAT IS AOC/AOP?

Currently, three different categories of wine are defined by the European Union wine regulations:

• *Vin sans indication géographique* (VSIG) or Wine without geographical indication, formerly known as "Vin de table" (Table wine). This category is now mentioned on the label as "Vin" (wine) followed by the name of the producing member state; for instance "Vin de France" (Wine from France) when the grapes are harvested and vinified on the national territory. This mention may be completed by indications of grape variety and/or vintage.

• *Vin avec IGP/Indication géographique protégée* (PGI or Protected Geographical Indication) — this is the European term; the French term is *Vin de pays*. These wines are produced from grapes harvested in a department or in a specified production zone, in accordance with legally defined production conditions, and vinified in the same department or zone. For instance, Vin de pays de l'Atlantique is a PGI.

• *Vin AOP/AOC* (AOP/AOC Wine): the European term is AOP (DPO or Protected Designation of Origin in English), but in France, AOC (*Appellation d'origine contrôlée*) is accepted as a mention in the commercial denomination. A wine may be entitled to AOC status if it answers some strict conditions of production, winemaking and commercialization as defined by the AOC specifications established by the ODG (Defense and management organization), validated by INAO (National Institute for Origin and Quality), and published in the French *Journal officiel*. Technically, it is controlled by OI (Inspection organizations) and OC (Certification organizations) that regularly control the operators (producers, winemakers, wine traders…), particularly on precise production criteria such as appellation zone (always exactly delineated), grape varieties, yield, alcoholic degree, or agricultural and winemaking methods, etc.

This mention should imperatively be in French and composed of the name of the appellation (a region, or a village) followed by the mention "Appellation d'origine contrôlée/protégée" or "Appellation X contrôlée/protégée".

Bordeaux has 60 AOC/AOP; some exist both as red wine and as white wine appellations, while others allow just one or the other.

It should be noted — and this is also an extra guarantee for the consumer — that no AOC/AOP is given to a wine for a limitless period of time. Every year, the producer or trader has to renew his request for the new harvest, and his products as well as his production tools are tested.

BORDEAUX IS...

• 113,400 hectares of AOC vines.
• 5.25 million hectoliters of AOC wines produced in 2012, thus 700 million bottles.
• A turnover of 4.2 billion euros.
• 60 AOC (*Appellation d'origine contrôlée* or DPO).
• 7,375 wine growers/winemakers including 92% AOC, 89 wine brokers, 300 trading houses, 36 cooperative wineries, four cooperative unions, and 55,000 jobs, directly or indirectly connected to winemaking.
• 58% of the Bordeaux wine production goes to the French market, 42% is exported.
• 23 bottles of Bordeaux wine are sold every second in the world.

IN FRANCE:

• Nearly two thirds of the total volume of Bordeaux wines are marketed in France, including one third in cafés, hotels and restaurants.
• Nearly one out of two French households buys Bordeaux wines for home consumption.
• Supermarkets and hypermarkets remain key players in the distribution of Bordeaux wines, especially through seasonal wine fairs.

BORDEAUX AS A EUROPEAN WINE REGION:
THE RECENT CHANGES

FORMER DENOMINATION	NEW DENOMINATION	COMMENTS
TABLE WINES (VINS DE TABLE)	Wines without geographical indication (vins sans IG)	Wines without geographical indication are the first category updated by the new regulations.
VINS DE PAYS	IGP wines (PGI, Protected Geographical Indication)	IGPs and AOPs are gathered under the category of wines with geographical indication, the second category updated by the new regulations.
AOC (Appellation d'origine contrôlée)	AOP (PDO, Protected Designation of Origin)	

2
BORDEAUX

BORDEAUX, *THE IDENTITY OF* A WINE REGION

The wines of Bordeaux have a strong identity, through a wide range of styles and colors. In Bordeaux, wine is first and foremost based on balance, the natural result of excellent winemaking and the art of blending. Sensorial as well as spiritual pleasure are also closely connected to that balance. Bordeaux also means a very special lifestyle, and a city that is currently recovering its rightful rank among great world destinations.

BORDEAUX CITY, HEART OF THE VINEYARD

The city of Bordeaux lies at the heart of its wine region. Far beyond its natural role as the center of the winemaking activity, it is also the very image and symbol of that region. The sight of the Graves vineyard, at the very limits of the city, is a strong reminder of that reality. For many centuries, Bordeaux has been thinking wine and breathing wine. (See "Bordeaux, the birth of a legend", pages 30 and 31.)

During the 20th century, the facades on the docks bordering the Garonne, blackened by time and harbor soot, were showing their age. Over the last ten years, extensive renovations have been carried out and the beautiful classic buildings have now regained their former grace. The river banks that have witnessed, over the centuries, so many goods being disembarked and so many barrels of wine being shipped have been cleaned and restored. The gold-colored 17th and 18th-century limestone facades adorned

THE BORDEAUX VINEYARD

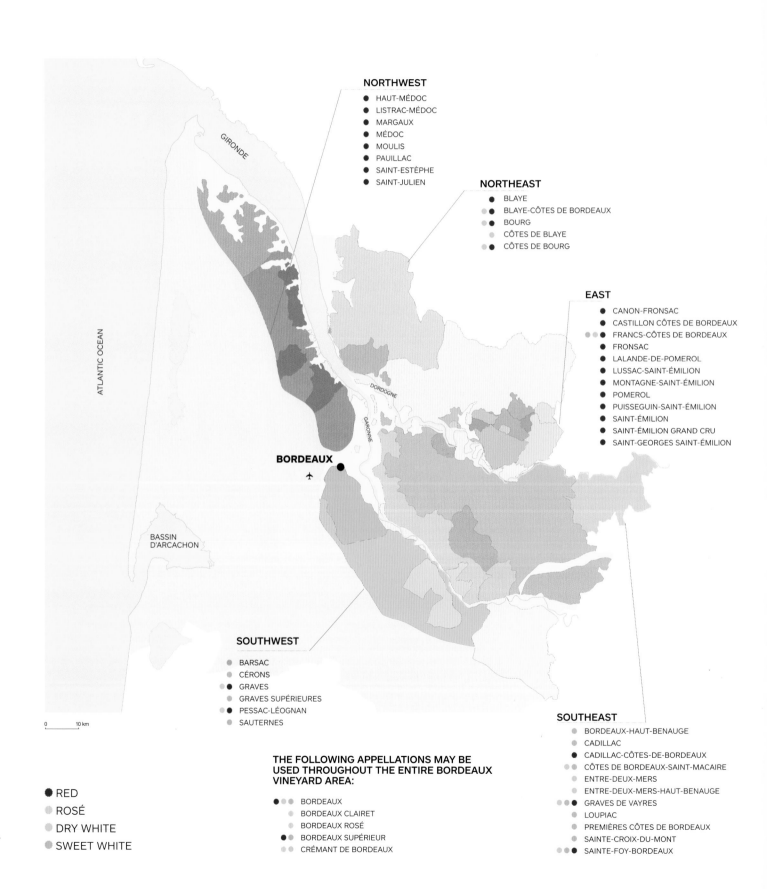

NORTHWEST
- HAUT-MÉDOC
- LISTRAC-MÉDOC
- MARGAUX
- MÉDOC
- MOULIS
- PAUILLAC
- SAINT-ESTÈPHE
- SAINT-JULIEN

NORTHEAST
- BLAYE
- BLAYE-CÔTES DE BORDEAUX
- BOURG
- CÔTES DE BLAYE
- CÔTES DE BOURG

EAST
- CANON-FRONSAC
- CASTILLON CÔTES DE BORDEAUX
- FRANCS-CÔTES DE BORDEAUX
- FRONSAC
- LALANDE-DE-POMEROL
- LUSSAC-SAINT-ÉMILION
- MONTAGNE-SAINT-ÉMILION
- POMEROL
- PUISSEGUIN-SAINT-ÉMILION
- SAINT-ÉMILION
- SAINT-ÉMILION GRAND CRU
- SAINT-GEORGES SAINT-ÉMILION

GIRONDE

ATLANTIC OCEAN

DORDOGNE

GARONNE

BORDEAUX ●

BASSIN D'ARCACHON

SOUTHWEST
- BARSAC
- CÉRONS
- GRAVES
- GRAVES SUPÉRIEURES
- PESSAC-LÉOGNAN
- SAUTERNES

0   10 km

SOUTHEAST
- BORDEAUX-HAUT-BENAUGE
- CADILLAC
- CADILLAC-CÔTES-DE-BORDEAUX
- CÔTES DE BORDEAUX-SAINT-MACAIRE
- ENTRE-DEUX-MERS
- ENTRE-DEUX-MERS-HAUT-BENAUGE
- GRAVES DE VAYRES
- LOUPIAC
- PREMIÈRES CÔTES DE BORDEAUX
- SAINTE-CROIX-DU-MONT
- SAINTE-FOY-BORDEAUX

THE FOLLOWING APPELLATIONS MAY BE USED THROUGHOUT THE ENTIRE BORDEAUX VINEYARD AREA:
- BORDEAUX
- BORDEAUX CLAIRET
- BORDEAUX ROSÉ
- BORDEAUX SUPÉRIEUR
- CRÉMANT DE BORDEAUX

- ● RED
- ● ROSÉ
- ● DRY WHITE
- ● SWEET WHITE

THE CITÉ DES CIVILISATIONS DU VIN

This major project, scheduled to open in 2016, aims to provide Bordeaux with a cultural showcase around the theme of wine. As innovative in its architecture as it is in terms of content, La Cité will offer an exploratory journey through vineyards, time and the civilizations of wine on an area of 14,000 square meters on the banks of the Garonne, past the newly renovated docks.

Designed by the French-British architects' office X-TU (Paris)/Casson Mann (London), the site will include a permanent "multisensory" journey through twenty-three wine-related themes organized in six modules: At the Heart of Civilization, The Imaginary Worlds of Wine, Bordeaux, Wine and You, Vineyards of the World, and From the Vine to the Glass. It will also house a panoramic restaurant, tasting workshops, an auditorium and temporary exhibition rooms. 420,000 visitors per year are expected.

For more information: www.centrecultureleduvin.com

with the famous Bordeaux mascarons are now visible in their original state. The same renovation works have seen the traffic system redesigned and regulated so that pedestrians can fully enjoy the urban and riverside landscape again. Facing the magnificent architectural ensemble of the Place de la Bourse, built between 1730 and 1775 by Ange-Jacques Gabriel, architect to the King of France, there now stands the *Miroir d'eau* — a wide, shallow pool of water in which the changing skies of this estuary region are reflected. In the Summer, visitors come there to cool their feet and play while admiring the wonderful harmony of the river, the sky and the city's skyline.

A Unesco World Heritage city since 2007, Bordeaux greets an ever-growing number of tourists. Its easy and attractive lifestyle is easily explained by the combination of a mild climate, generous natural conditions, proximity to the Ocean and the meeting of two major rivers. With its many wine shops, cafés, museums and art galleries, and a large number of restaurants (as the French city with the highest ratio of restaurants per capita), Bordeaux epitomizes the union of wine and gastronomy. From high-end dining to country-style bistro, from *entrecôte bordelaise* to lamprey stewed in red wine, not to forget oysters from the Bassin d'Arcachon, and even some Sichuan cuisine, there are many opportunities to sample the local wines alongside a good meal.

Being open to the world is another important aspect of Bordelais culture. The city has always been hospitable. The origin of family names in the local wine trade and even in winemaking leaves no doubt about it: the citizens of Bordeaux come from everywhere. From all regions of France and particularly of Gascony, obviously, but also from England, Ireland, Scandinavia, Holland, Austria, Spain or Portugal… If, on one hand, it is undeniable that the Bordeaux wine trade emerged as an aristocratic elite in the 17th century, on the other hand it must be pointed out that this elite is based on the right of soil as much as on the right of blood. Throughout its history, Bordeaux partly built itself from the many immigrants seeking their fortune, or coming for a temporary stay that the appeal of the city turned into a permanent one: the Bartons, Kirwans, Lurtons from Ireland; the Schylers from Austria, the Cruses from Denmark… This openness of mind is instrumental, now as ever, in maintaining the city's unique atmosphere and energy.

A few days in Bordeaux, with a few trips selected in a rich and varied program offered by the various local tourist organizations (see page 28), will quickly convince the visitor that their initiation to wine and to the typical Bordeaux harmony is no less than an initiation to pleasure.

THE BORDEAUX CHÂTEAU

No description of Bordeaux wines could be complete without explaining the notion of "wine château".

The term "château" in the context of the Bordeaux vineyard means both the wine estate in its entirety and the building that is meant to house the owner's family. The vast majority of wines made in the Gironde are named after a château, but there are a few exceptions: for instance Petrus, the famous Pomerol growth, or Clos-Haut-Peyraguey, a first classified growth of Sauternes.

While it is true that, in the Gironde, most wine châteaux were built after the 17th century, some older buildings were châteaux, or castles, in the architectural sense of the term before becoming wine châteaux. For instance, Château d'Yquem, in Sauternes, has been known for its wines since the end of the 16th century, but the fortress itself was built in Medieval times. This is also the case of Château La Tour-Carnet in the Médoc. However, wine châteaux did not become common in the Bordelais until the mid-18th century, with a massive building period starting in the second half of the 19th century, after the 1855 Classification.

Many different architectural styles can be found across the Bordeaux vineyard, from the graceful *chartreuse* (a local term for a small 18th-century mansion) to the simple and elegant Girondine house or the Neoclassic palace. After 1855, the château often became a display window for its owner's ambitions, and there was a profusion of Neo-Gothic and Neo-Renaissance styles. Sometimes, the inspiration was more exotic, as in the "Chinese" pagodas of Château Cos-d'Estournel in Saint-Estèphe.

This does not mean that the Bordeaux château, as a rule, indulges in ostentation. Many wine châteaux are relatively small, and in some cases, the name even applies to a simple family house or a farm house. More often than not, the architect has applied his talent to the winemaking facilities (vat rooms or cellars) as well as to the château: you may see such architectural programs at Château Margaux, at Château Pontet-Canet (Pauillac), or at Château Malescot-Saint-Exupéry (Margaux), where a visit of the entire estate is recommended.

Today, the Bordeaux châteaux owners are still taking good care of their architectural heritage, being quite aware of the aesthetic appeal of a beautiful barrel cellar or vat house. Some châteaux, particularly of classified growths, have entrusted the renovation of their cellars to some great names of architecture and design. This is a trend that contributes greatly to the development of wine tourism in the Gironde. Naturally, you may visit those wonders, by appointment or through the wine tourism platforms men-

tioned on page 28 ("The keys to wine tourism"). In 2009, architect Jean-Michel Wilmotte installed a set of brushed steel tronconical vats in the old walls of Château Cos-d'Estournel, giving the entire place a futuristic look. The new cellar (2011) of Château Cheval-Blanc, designed by Christian de Portzamparc, is a large white ellipse that gives the visual impression of hovering weightlessly over the vines. Among the most recently renovated cellars is that of Château Mouton-Rothschild, designed by Bernard Mazières, with 64 vats arranged in a striking perspective. Most of the vats are made of wood, a few of stainless steel; all are set in the imposing oakwood framework of a cathedral-like structure, supported by riveted steel pillars. These are only a few of the many wonderful sights to discover in the Bordeaux vineyard.

WINE TOURISM: THE ROADS OF WINE

The best way to learn about Bordeaux wines is to discover them right on the spot. With 4.3 million visitors per year, including 31% from overseas, the Gironde is the most popular destination for wine tourism in France. One of the main goals of wine tourists is to visit vineyards; tasting and buying wines is another.

For easier access to the vineyards, in addition to the wine tourism platforms available on the Internet, an increasing number of wine châteaux have their own website and open their doors to visitors (not all need appointments, but it is best to check ahead).

There are many tourist routes all over the entire region, from which you can discover:

– In the Northwest (Médoc), on the Route des Châteaux, which runs through the peninsula from south to north, the numerous wine châteaux of the Médoc — among them the Great Classified Growths of 1855 — and their architectural diversity.

– To the North (Bourg, Blaye), on the Route des Coteaux, along the estuary, the round, fruity wines produced in the shade of Romanesque church steeples.

– To the East, around Saint-Émilion, Pomerol and Fronsac, on the Route du Patrimoine, wines of international fame, and World heritage villages.

– To the Southeast (Entre-Deux-Mers, Bordeaux), along the Route des Bastides, dry white wines to be enjoyed in all their freshness.

– To the Southwest (Graves, Sauternes), on the Route des Graves, bordering the Landes forest, varied terroirs produce a subtle variation of red, dry white and sweet white wines.

THE KEYS TO WINE TOURISM

BORDEAUX WINE TRIP
To help you find your way through multiple offers, the vast surface of the vineyard and the cultural richness of the wine world, Bordeaux Wine Trip, created in partnership with the CIVB (Interprofessional Council of Bordeaux wines) and the CRT (Regional Committee of Aquitaine Tourism) is a smartphone or tablet application with the addition of a website. It can be used to find all the wine tourism offers near your current location with just a few clicks, and the user may organize their own itinerary by creating their own road map.

SMART BORDEAUX
Another free application for smartphone or tablet (also accessible through a website), Smart Bordeaux greatly facilitates the access to the world of Bordeaux wines. Just scan the bottle (via the label, barcode or 2D code) and Smart Bordeaux provides you with all practical information, provided by wine growers and wine traders: name of château, appellation, color of wine, grape varieties, awards (medals, ratings), *cuvées*, soil and winemaking characteristics, accessibility to visitors. Users can comment on the bottles and post to social networks. Smart Bordeaux can also suggest a selection of several suitable wines after certain criteria (color, taste profile, DPO) have been entered.

WINE TOURISM — A FEW LINKS
www.bordeauxwinetrip.com
www.smart-bordeaux.com
www.bordeaux-tourisme.fr, the website of the Bordeaux Tourist Office
www.oenoland-aquitaine.fr
www.tourisme-gironde.fr and the Vignobles et Chais en Bordelais charter
www.tourisme-aquitaine.fr and the Destination Vignobles label

BORDEAUX, THE BIRTH OF A LEGEND

FIRST CLARET, FIRST COMMERCIAL GROWTH

Although the origins of Bordeaux wine date back to Gallo-Roman times, it was in the Middle Ages that the vineyard of the Gironde became a model of commercial and oenological excellence.

In 1152, Eleanor, Duchess of Aquitaine, married Henry Plantagenet, the future king of England. From then on, trade connections were created between Aquitaine and the British Isles. The British exported food, fabrics, metals, and imported Bordeaux wines, of which they were very fond. They named them *clarets* because of their lightness and delicacy.

The shipping of wines by sea was facilitated by the size of the English fleet and by the easy access to the port of Bordeaux through the Gironde estuary; both allowed for a significant expansion of the Bordeaux vineyards. At that time, wine was shipped in barrels with a capacity of 900 liters (equaling four 225-liter Bordeaux barrels of today). That type of barrel later became the international volume unit for ship gauging. However, this trade flow was interrupted in 1453 by the conquest of Aquitaine by the French army.

THE ROLE OF THE DUTCH, AND THE NEW FRENCH CLARET

In the 17th century, a new era of prosperity began for the Bordeaux vineyard with the emergence of new commercial outlets: the Dutch, the Hanseatic League and the Britons. This changing distribution meant deep changes in the very nature of the marketed wines, for the Dutch brought on quite different trade patterns from those of their English predecessors, with an emphasis, for instance, on the development of distilled spirits. Bordeaux traders then began to provide, in addition to their traditional clarets, some dry white wines and sweet white wines for distillation. At the same time, a drainage of the Médoc land was undertaken by Dutch engineers, a measure that later allowed the cultivation of vines on the peninsula. Finally, the Dutch introduced in Bordeaux the practice of burning sulfur within the oak barrels to clean and disinfect them, ensuring ensure a better conservation of wines during aging and shipping.

Also at the end of that century, a new type of red wine appeared in Bordeaux, created by Arnaud III de Pontac on his estate of Haut-Brion in Pessac: he had noticed that growing vines in poor, gravelly soil produced a fuller-bodied, more densely colored wine that could be kept much longer. Previously, clarets were produced in clayey soils near rivers (*palus*). This New French Claret was instantly popular in England and paved the way for the revival of Bordeaux wine that started in the 18th century.

THE ISLES OF AMERICA

In the 18th century, the islands of America — Santo Domingo and the Lesser Antilles — ensured the growth of Bordeaux wine exports, and Bordeaux prospered on that colonial trade until the French Revolution. By then, England as an export market for Gironde wines had dropped to only 10% of the bulk, but it was instrumental in making fine, full-bodied wines with good aging power fashionable in London high society.

At the same period, the first corked and sealed bottles started to appear. This new type of glass vessel gradually replaced the barrel in overseas shipments.

CRISES AND PROSPERITY

In the first years of the 19th century, the overall situation of the Gironde vineyard was essentially characterized by a state of deep commercial stagnation. Later, towards the middle of the century, a terrible fungal disease called powdery mildew hit the vineyard. First observed in England in 1845, it appeared in the Bordeaux region for the first time around 1851. In 1857, a remedy was discovered in the form of sulfur spraying. Once the danger of mildew was averted, the Gironde regained its former prosperity.

Also in the mid-19th century, at the request of Emperor Napoleon III, a classification of the most reputable growths of the Left Bank of the Gironde (Médoc, Sauternais and Château Haut-Brion in the Graves) was published. It was the famous 1855 classification, which more or less exactly overlapped the rave tasting reviews of Thomas Jefferson, the future President of the United States who, more than half a century before, had come to Bordeaux to collect the material for one of the first wine cellars in the White House.

Two decades later, a new threat, the phylloxera crisis (1875-1892), appeared on the horizon. The introduction of American vine plants contaminated by a small insect called phylloxera wiped the French vineyard almost entirely. The Bordeaux vineyard was finally rescued by the grafting of French grape varieties on phylloxera-resistant American rootstocks, a process that was extended to all French vineyards. However, the remedy provided its own share of disease, for mildew, yet another calamity, followed phylloxera. Ultimately, that fungus was kept in control by the discovery of the famous Bordeaux mixture, a mix of slaked lime and copper sulfate.

AN ERA OF REGULATIONS

As the 20th century approached, the entire French vineyard experienced a severe crisis characterized by fraud and falling prices. In order to protect themselves, the authorities of Gironde took part in 1911 in the development of a national legislation aiming at highlighting the origins of wines. The legislation defined areas of appellation of Bordeaux wines that excluded any other department than the Gironde. Initially imperfect and poorly enforced —World War I was just beginning—, this regulation was reinstated in 1936 after the creation of INAO, the National Institute of (Protected) Appellations of Origin. To the concept of origin was added that of quality control in the form of AOC (DPO or Appellation d'origine contrôlée), which represents 98% of Bordeaux's wine production.

New classifications were created, first for Graves, then for Saint-Émilion. After the dreadful frost of 1956, Bordeaux regained its prosperity, the nobility of its wines placing it in a worldwide leadership position.

Much appreciated in the 17th century, New French Claret was the prototype of modern Bordeaux red wines.

A UNIQUE
ACTIVITY SECTOR

VITICULTURE

During the last forty years, the Bordeaux vineyard has been experiencing an increased concentration of wine properties and trading structures. In 2013, the total number of wine growers amounted to 7,375 for an average surface area of 17 hectares of planted vines by exploitation. However, this is only an average figure that reflects only partially a more complex reality, which varies in different parts of the vineyard.

These wine growers are organized in several types of structures:

• Vertical organizations (wine unions, the Federation of Bordeaux Wines...).

• Horizontal organizations such as federated wine unions or syndicates (ODG — Defense and Management Organization), groups of producers, or the region's 36 cooperative wineries.

The cooperative wineries play an important part in three areas:

• Quality, ensuring the control of upstream processes (vine training, pruning, planting, input selection).

• Economy, by playing a role in market organization through the amount of produced wines and their storage capacities.

• Society, contributing to rural development (maintaining small family farms, creating jobs).

The model of the Bordeaux wine industry most notably the interactions between châteaux and traders has no equivalent in the world. Underneath an apparent complexity lies an richly intricate and authentic culture, and a three-centuries old tradition that is still as energetic now as it ever was. The world of Bordeaux wines is a subtle mix of heritage and modernity, of fidelity to the past and openness to the world. Without doubt, the close connections between the families of winemakers and traders help to explain that reality.

BROKERAGE

A broker, or courtier, is an important intermediary between winemakers and wine traders. He connects offer and demand according to wine quality, volume and desired price; he also does counseling and works out conciliation between parties. When the transaction is successful, he produces a sales confirmation certificate stating the exact conditions of the transaction.

The broker is morally responsible for the proper execution of the contract. Indeed, he has to watch over the wines until they are delivered and he has to make sure, through tasting and testing, that the delivered wines are in conformity with the samples previously presented. Finally, he never makes a deal for his own profit. As a remuneration for his work, he gets a broker's fee or *courtage* which amounts to 2% of the price agreed upon by both parties. This fee is generally paid by the buyer.

Some brokers may be recognized as official specialists into the authenticity of wines. When they are, they can be summoned at auctions or for expertise. They also establish the official pricing of wines following the transactions made in the Bordeaux market. Because of their skills, they are generally summoned to assess the quality of some wines or to list them hierarchically in order to achieve a ranking or classification.

TRADING

Wine trading in the Bordeaux region is strong and diversified, and rooted in an age-old tradition: 300 companies of various size and structure are gathered around the wine unions of Libourne and Bordeaux. More than two-thirds of Bordeaux wines are marketed by the Gironde traders who are also responsible for over 80% of exports to 170 countries. The 2012-2013 turnover of the Gironde wine traders was of around 3 billion euros.

Through its commercial dynamism, trading is a particularly effective actor in the regional economy and in the international reputation of Bordeaux. Interestingly, the sector's concentration has been steadily increasing for the past fifteen years — in 2012, the biggest 46 companies produced 94% of the overall turnover. The wine trader, or *négociant*, by establishing the necessary connection between winemaker and consumer, is an important link in the chain of the wine industry. He buys wines and sells them to every circuit of distribution (supermarkets, wine shops, cafés, restaurants, etc.) and to all markets, in France and abroad. Each trader has its own specificities, from small-producer wines to classified growths. Some trading houses select, develop and bottle wines under their own label: these are called branded wines. Some families divide their activities between trade and winemaking.

A trader usually plays a double role:
• He practices the traditional business of selling selected wines (usually châteaux wines produced and bottled at the estate).
• He is engaged in the important activity of storing and aging wines marketed under brand names. Wines are purchased in bulk, blended, aged and offered under brands that bring to consumers the guarantee of their expertise and to distributors a steady supply.

The economic role of wine trading is related to its annual bottling capacity (about 650 million bottles) and storage capacity (600 million bottles), and therefore to its ability to regulate the market, protecting it against price fluctuation. It should also be noted that the technologies and processes they set up in their conditioning structures may entitle them to the certifications required by French and international distribution from its suppliers (IFS, BRC, ISO, etc.), thus guaranteeing proper packaging, traceability, hygiene and food safety.

WINE PROFESSIONS

COMMUNICATION
PR
EVENTS
ADVERTISING

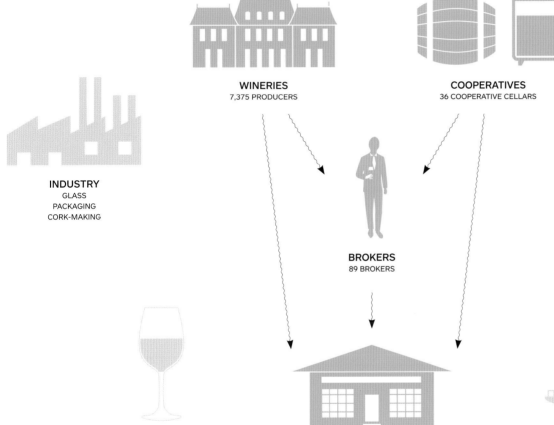

WINERIES
7,375 PRODUCERS

COOPERATIVES
36 COOPERATIVE CELLARS

INDUSTRY
GLASS
PACKAGING
CORK-MAKING

DISTRIBUTION
SUPERMARKETS
WINE MERCHANTS
HORECA AND
OTHER CATERING
BUSINESSES

BROKERS
89 BROKERS

WINE TOURISM

TRADERS
300 TRADING HOUSES

EXPORT
FREIGHT

RESEARCH
EDUCATION

THE MAGICAL
EQUATION OF
BORDEAUX WINES

The specificity of Bordeaux wines rests on two factors: the notion of blending, and a magical equation based on a simple principle: wine is the product of the interaction of climate, terroir, grape varieties and the work of men.

THE NOTIONS
OF GROWTH AND TERROIR

There are many microclimates in the Gironde. Highly localized by definition, they are the result of the interaction of climate with different sites in the Bordeaux region characterized by angle of slope, exposure to the sun, and topography. For the vine plant, the combination of these microclimates with the highly diversified types of soil found in the Bordeaux region creates the famous terroirs, or surrounding environments on limited surfaces.

The quality of these terroirs is expressed through the individual characteristics of the local grape varieties and through the way these varieties adapt to the place where they grow, and bring out its nuances. The result of that expression, in Bordeaux, is commonly called a *cru*, or growth.

The word *cru*, frequently seen on Bordeaux wine labels, reflects the quality level produced by the association of terroir, grape variety, and the winemaker's skills, and gives voice to that association.

CLIMATE AND TOPOGRAPHY: A PRIVILEGED SITUATION

Bordering the Atlantic Ocean and exactly situated on the 45th north parallel — halfway between the North pole and the equator —, the vineyard of Bordeaux is entirely contained within the administrative subdivision (department) of the Gironde, enjoying an extremely pleasant situation and climate.

The topography of the Gironde includes three distinct regions:

• To the West, on the left bank of the Garonne, from the Graves to the Médoc, a plateau that gently slopes towards the coastline.

• To the East, on the right bank of the Dordogne, a rolling plateau (100 to 130 meters high), mostly hilly with relatively deep valleys, but no steep slopes or sharp relief. From coast to coast, it stretches between Castillon-la-Bataille and Blaye.

• Between these two regions, delimited by two rivers, the Entre-Deux-Mers is a hilly region where the highest points of the department are located. The local hydrography, evidently based on the Garonne and the Dordogne, also rests on an abundant network of small streams that naturally meets, every year, in normal conditions, the water needs of the Bordeaux vineyard.

The climate of the Bordeaux region is of a mild oceanic type. It benefits, on the one hand, from the influence of the Gulf Stream — a warm water stream from the Caribbean region that runs along the coast of Aquitaine, warming and regulating the local temperatures —, and on the other hand from the influence of the Landes forest, a wide stretch of pine trees acting as an effective protective screen against the Atlantic winds and tempering the classic oceanic climate. The combination of all these factors results in a largely pleasant climate that greatly favors the optimal ripening of grapes, with sunny Summers, mild Falls, very little frost in Winter and relatively damp Springs. The only climatic incidents feared by winemakers are:

• Spring frosts while the vine is flowering and cold rains during the pollination, for these may induce *coulure* or shatter, which happens when pollens, dragged to the ground by rain and wind, fail to come in contact with the flowers and fertilize them. Some grape varieties are more prone to coulure than others.

• Hail, which may cause severe damage to the vine plant at any point until harvest time, affecting flowers, fruits, shoots or leaves.

TERROIRS

For the planting of an excellent vineyard, the quality of soil is a crucial element. Anchored to a limestone subsoil covered with siliceous and gravelly-sandy deposits, the Bordeaux vineyard has a geologic diversity that particularly favors wine-growing and the production of extremely diversified wines.

• On the left bank of the Garonne and of the Gironde estuary (Médoc, Graves, Sauternes), the soils are mostly gravelly, of variable thicknesses, a result of the erosion of the Pyrenées by the Garonne and at some places, in the Médoc, of the Massif Central by the Dordogne river, during thousands of years. These soils are composed of pebbles, gravels and sands carried throughout the interglacial periods. They have great filtering abilities and are also very good for absorbing and accumulating heat, which helps with the grapes' ripening. Indeed the hard stone pebbles that constitute most of the *graves* (gravelly) soils absorb the heat during the day and radiate it back to the plants during the night.

• On the right bank of the Dordogne (the Libourne region, Saint-Émilion, Pomerol, Fronsac, Blayais, Côtes de Bordeaux…), a whole palette of soils of varying compositions can be found. They directly come from the erosion of several types of source rocks, which include clays, limestone, sands, and some gravel. With their relatively fine texture, these soils have the ability to absorb and retain rain water, which helps to cool the vines. Nevertheless, since they are generally situated on top of hills and endowed with good drainage capacity, they let excess water seep down to the deeper layers of soil, where it is not likely to smother the vine's roots.

• Between Garonne and Dordogne (Entre-Deux-Mers, Loupiac, Cadillac, Sainte-Croix-du-Mont…), the soils are essentially clay-limestone, which means that they are cool and humid, like some of the right bank of the Dordogne.

It should also be noted that the nature of soil is directly connected to the mineral components drawn in by the vine's roots and transferred, ultimately, into the composition of the grape juice. Thus, in Bordeaux, it is possible to find, on radically different soils, vineyards producing equally successful wines with extremely varied organoleptic qualities — that is the magic of these great soils.

GRAPE VARIETIES

On the many painstakingly studied and cultivated terroirs of the Bordeaux vineyard, grape varieties are planted. Their adaptation to their environment is also the result of an age-old traditional knowledge.

RED GRAPE VARIETIES

• The most common red grape variety is merlot, which covers a little more than 69,400 hectares. A precocious, vigorous type of vine, it can express its potential qualities in most Bordelais soils, but it prefers the cool and humid nature of clay-textured soils. It ripens easily and is generally the first to do so, while being vulnerable to grey rot and coulure (shatter), especially in silty soils. Merlot brings to wines color, alcoholic content, suppleness and roundness in the tannic structure, and plenty of aromatic elegance. Not predominant on the left bank of the Garonne, it predominates in right bank plantings, particularly in Pomerol. It brings aromatic notes of fleshy red fruits, plum, fig — and, after a few years of bottle aging, some toasted notes.

• Cabernet sauvignon, the most traditional grape in the Bordeaux vineyard (covering about 26,000 hectares), is a late-ripening, small-berried and thick-skinned variety that is particularly well adapted to the gravelly, warm and dry soils of the left bank of the Garonne. It is resistent to grey rot and produces a regular, moderate yield of fruit. As a young wine, it is very aromatic, providing a tannic richness and power suitable for long aging, at the end of which the patient amateur is rewarded by distinctive wines with a rich, complex and harmonious flavor, reminiscent of black fruit (blackcurrant, blackberry) and licorice, developing undergrowth notes after some years. It is predominant on the left bank and more infrequent on the right bank.

• Cabernet franc (about 12,000 hectares) is mostly grown in the Libournais. It ripens slightly earlier than cabernet sauvignon. The wines that are extracted from its small berries are rich in polyphenols, and much appreciated for their aromatic finesse and aging qualities. With a very expressive nose and a strong tannic structure, cabernet franc gives notes of raspberry and violet. Generally not dominant in Bordeaux blends, it can be the main variety in some Saint-Émilion wines.

• Three other varieties, known as "auxiliary" grapes, are far less common: malbec (also known as côt, pressac, or auxerrois), petit verdot and carmenère. They are generally present in blending in small proportions.

THE GRAPE VARIETIES OF BORDEAUX

Red grape varieties   88% of planted area
• 65% merlot
• 23% cabernet sauvignon
• 10% cabernet franc
• 2% other varieties such as malbec, petit verdot, carmenère...

White grape varieties   12% of planted area
• 49% sémillon
• 43% sauvignon
• 6% muscadelle
• 2% other varieties such as colombard, ugni blanc, sauvignon gris, merlot blanc...

THE NOTION OF GRAPE VARIETY IN FRANCE

All the grape varieties grown in France belong to the *Vitis vinifera* species. In France, four main families of grapes are defined according to the usual maturity date of chasselas (the reference variety). They have to be adapted to the climate and soils of any given wine-growing region. The four families comprise:

- Early varieties, which ripen from eight to ten days before chasselas. Their cultivation zone is located in the northern regions of France.
- First-period varieties, which ripen more or less at the same time as chasselas. Their cultivation zone covers Alsace, Champagne and Burgundy.
- Second-period varieties, which ripen from twelve to fifteen days after chasselas. Their cultivation zones are Alsace, Val de Loire, Bordeaux, the Southwest and the northern Côtes du Rhône.
- Third-period varieties, ripening from twenty to thirty days after chasselas. Their cultivation zone is the South of France.

Varieties are also classified according to four major zones defined by two climatic gradients — air hygrometry and temperature. Grape varieties that are sensitive to these two limiting factors are generally located in one particular region (for instance riesling in Alsace or mourvèdre in the Midi); but the varieties that are only vulnerable to one of the two factors may be found on a whole half of the French territory (for instance: sauvignon and cabernets in the West; ugni blanc in the South).

WHITE GRAPE VARIETIES

• Sémillon (about 7,300 hectares) is a much appreciated variety that is well rooted in the Gironde, particularly in zones where sweet white wines are produced — there, sémillon wines are golden-colored, delicate, rich and extremely smooth. To dry white wines, it brings aromatic elegance and smoothness, with notes of apricot, acacia blossoms and almond. When it is enhanced by noble rot (*Botrytis cinerea*, see "Sweet Bordeaux" on page 67), it develops very special fragrances (candied fruits, dried fruits). It is the major variety in *liquoreux* and *moelleux* wines, and dominates in Sauternes plantings. It is used as a minor component of dry whites.

• Sauvignon blanc (about 5,500 hectares) is the major reference for the production of dry white wines. Giving an excellent expression of terroir, it brings plenty of liveliness, minerality, good acidity and aromatic potential. It produces pale yellow-colored dry white wines with a powerful, fruity bouquet, with notes of citrus, box tree, fig leaf, and sometimes a slight smoky note. More or less a minority variety in *moelleux* and *liquoreux* wines, it is dominant in dry whites.

• Muscadelle (about 870 hectares) has a predilection for clay soils where it is less vulnerable to rot than in shallow, well drained soils. Wines made from it are very aromatic, round and slightly musky, with low acidity and powerful, floral notes. It is frequently used in small proportion in *moelleux* and *liquoreux* Bordeaux blends.

• Like the reds, white wines also have their auxiliary varieties — colombard, merlot blanc, sauvignon gris and ugni blanc.

MAN'S WORK:
THE ART OF BLENDING

Unlike some other French or non-French vineyards that produce only monovarietal wines, Bordeaux has the particularity of producing mostly blended wines, obtained from more than one variety. Indeed, each major Bordelais grape variety has its own characteristics, which it develops in the course of its growth and maturing process (minerals from the subsoil, sunlight, freshness, character…). The specificity of Bordeaux wines is the direct result of skilful control of the complementary natures and mutual interaction of these grape varieties. The specific aromas of each variety are wonderfully matched together like colors on a master painter's canvas.

In Bordeaux, blending is a centuries-old tradition and an art in its own right, passed down and perfected by generations of cellar masters. They have long known that a dry white wine will rely on the freshness, the aromatic power and the aging qualities of a sauvignon, that a liquoreux needs the richness and elegance of sémillon, and that the faint exotic note of muscadelle can make all the difference in the same wine. They are also aware that merlot fares better on the cool limestone soils of the right bank, whereas cabernet sauvignon, which loves heat, has a liking for the warm, gravelly soils of the left bank. In a cabernet sauvignon-merlot blend, cabernet helps with merlot's keeping qualities by reinforcing its tannic structure, while merlot adds a softer touch to the association.

For more information, see the organoleptic descriptions of grape varieties in chapter 4, page 139.

The specific aromas of each grape variety are wonderfully matched together like colors on a master painter's canvas.

PLOT BY PLOT

Blending does not rely only on grape varieties. For many generations, Bordeaux winemakers have known that each plot has its own particular character and that the secret of a successful blending lies in organizing the winemaking, then the blending, according to these different qualities. For this reason, the grapes of each plot are, as often as possible, fermented separately or following the various local characteristics within the surface area of a wine estate.

Moreover, winemakers have learned to make use of subsoil quality. Centuries ago, wine growers had realized that, inside one particular plot, the vines fared differently from one zone to another, while neither the soil, the elevation or the exposition to the sun could come as an explanation for that. For a few years now, subsoil investigations and analyses have confirmed their observation by distinguishing radical mineral and hydrological differences, indiscernable on the surface but absorbed by the vine plant's long roots. For instance, some wines from Saint-Estèphe in the Médoc have a unique taste caused by the presence of a deep vein of blue clay, the same clay that is found in Pomerol.

This painstaking study of the plot structure has opened the way to ever-more precise vinification and an increased practice of fermenting in separate vats, either plot-by-plot or even sub-plot-by-subplot, in order to improve the blending even further. Thus, Bordeaux blending becomes a true master craftsmanship, producing an unmatched delicacy of taste.

COLORS AND AROMAS

TYPE OF WINE	COLOR EVOLUTION WITH AGING	AROMAS
BORDEAUX DRY WHITE WINES	Yellowish green --- > straw yellow	Lemon, grapefruit, white flowers, tropical fruits, mineral and flinty notes
SPARKLING BORDEAUX (crémants)	White or rosy, from pale to rusty pink	Citrus, white flowers, peach, lychee, plus a strawberry-raspberry note in rosés
SWEET BORDEAUX (moelleux and liquoreux white Bordeaux wines)	Pale gold --- > amber yellow, intense copper	Citrus peels, orange, pineapple, quince, apricot, honey
BORDEAUX ROSÉS AND CLAIRETS	Pale pink (rosé), raspberry pink (clairet) --- > deep 'onion skin' color	Strawberry, raspberry, redcurrant, cherry
BORDEAUX REDS WITH A MAJORITY OF MERLOT	Purplish red --- > warm red, after ruby and brick red phases	Cherry, blackberry, strawberry, violet
BORDEAUX REDS WITH A MAJORITY OF CABERNET SAUVIGNON	Purplish red --- > warm red, after ruby then brick red stages	Blackcurrant, black fruits, spices, mineral notes

THE COLORS OF BORDEAUX: AN INFINITE PALETTE OF SHADES

Owing to the vast surface area of the Bordeaux vineyard — and therefore to its many microclimates —, to the variety of its terroirs, and finally to the interaction of all those factors with the grape varietals, it is no wonder that Bordeaux wines come in a wide range of colors. The winemaker's action may be compared to that of an orchestra conductor composing an entire musical score from the natural elements he has at hand.

While it is true that the enthusiasm of English wine lovers, starting from the 17th century, was mostly reserved for red wines (New French Claret), the rich color palette of Bordeaux wines should not be overlooked — dry whites, sweet whites, rosés, clairets and reds… A palette whose colors also change and evolve with time. When associated with the different grape varietals and the various winemaking methods, this palette also reflects the even wider range of Bordeaux tastes and aromas, declined through the six families of Bordeaux wines (Bordeaux and Bordeaux Supérieur, Côtes de Bordeaux, Saint-Émilion-Pomerol-Fronsac, Médoc and Graves, Dry White Wines, Sweet Bordeaux).

THE SIX FAMILIES OF BORDEAUX WINES:
A MOSAIC OF
AOCs

Bordeaux owes its status as the largest AOC vineyard in France to the huge variety of its top-quality terroirs. In this vast choice of fine wines, every wine lover may find something to their liking – for every occasion, and in a wide range of prices. The six families of Bordeaux wines are defined by geographical factors and styles of wines.

BREAKDOWN OF THE SURFACE AREA OF THE BORDEAUX VINEYARD BY APPELLATION GROUPS

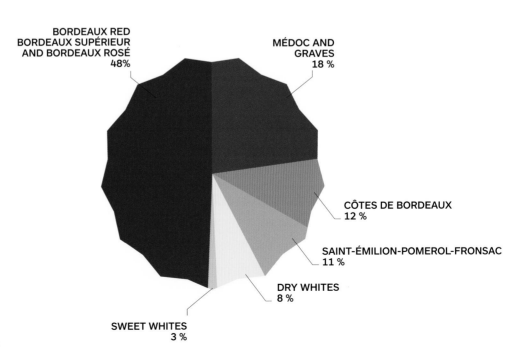

BORDEAUX RED
BORDEAUX SUPÉRIEUR
AND BORDEAUX ROSÉ
48%

MÉDOC AND
GRAVES
18 %

CÔTES DE BORDEAUX
12 %

SAINT-ÉMILION-POMEROL-FRONSAC
11 %

DRY WHITES
8 %

SWEET WHITES
3 %

SOURCE: CUSTOMS, 2013

BORDEAUX

AOCs PRODUCED ACROSS THE BORDEAUX VINEYARD AREA

Bordeaux (red, dry white and sweet white)
Bordeaux clairet
Bordeaux rosé
Bordeaux Supérieur (red and sweet white)
Bordeaux Crémant (sparkling rosé)

1

BORDEAUX ROUGE, BORDEAUX SUPÉRIEUR, BORDEAUX ROSÉ, AND BORDEAUX CLAIRET

BORDEAUX BRANDED WINES

Branded wines will often be found under these appellations. These are wines that are assembled in traders' cellars, according to specifications agreed upon by producer and trader. Consistency in quality, in price and in style are the most important criteria. The mere thought of Bordeaux instantly summons the image of the château. However, these brands, offering to consumers a reliable label and the entire commitment of a trading house to a specific product, are also a true expression of Bordeaux. Bordeaux châteaux and Bordeaux brands are complementary: indeed, the first Bordeaux wine brand of Bordeaux was created in the 1930s with Mouton-Cadet by Baron Philippe de Rothschild, the owner of Château Mouton Rothschild (First Classified Growth of Pauillac), thus paving the way to other quality brands of Bordeaux wines exported throughout the world.

THE FIVE AOCs OF BORDEAUX REDS, CLAIRETS AND ROSÉS

Bordeaux rouge, Bordeaux clairet, Bordeaux rosé, Bordeaux Supérieur (red), Crémant de Bordeaux (rosé). There is also a distilled spirit called Fine Bordeaux, under a regulated appellation.

The production of red wines in both Bordeaux and Bordeaux Supérieur appellations is allowed on the entire AOC territory within the limits of the department of the Gironde. These wines may therefore be produced on the right bank as well on the left bank, in many different soils and under a large variety of microclimates. The diversity of grapes and regions allows for the making of still wines (red, rosé or clairet) or sparkling wines (rosé); not to forget the production of a distilled eau-de-vie in the regulated Fine Bordeaux AOC. The individual character of these wines depends closely on the terroir on which they are made, and a certain standard of quality is a common feature of all these appellations.

Bordeaux and Bordeaux Supérieur rouges (reds) account for nearly half of the region's production. The production and wine-making constraints are stricter for Bordeaux Supérieur than for the simple Bordeaux appellation.

Bordeaux and Bordeaux Supérieur reds are primarily obtained from three varieties: merlot, cabernet sauvignon and cabernet franc. Merlot clearly dominates; the wines are therefore fruity, smooth, lively and balanced, with a distinctive aromatic freshness and, depending on the style, delicately oaky notes.

Bordeaux rosé and Bordeaux clairet are two distinct types of wine. The winemaking process for clairet is close to that of a light red wine, involving a short maceration time to extract some color and tannins. The maceration time for Bordeaux rosé is even shorter and is not followed by the secondary (softening) malo-lactic fermentation. All the typically Bordelais red grape varieties may be present in these wines, but cabernet franc and merlot are the most common.

Incidentally, the name *clairet* is likely to be at the origin of the English word claret, which has endured through the centuries to mean, in Britain, "red wine from Bordeaux", but *clairet* in the French sense is a particular type of wine produced in the Gironde. Crémants de Bordeaux have existed since 1990. They are sparkling wines, most frequently rosés, obtained from the traditional method of second fermentation in bottles, with a shorter time on slats than in Champagne.

CÔTES DE BORDEAUX (REDS)

The Côtes de Bordeaux AOC was created in 2008 in order to bring together a mosaic of small, highly individualized appellations under a strong and coherent identity. Thus, the vineyards of Côtes are located throughout the department, but they get their identity from a hilly landscape located along the right banks of the two major rivers. These vineyards share similar soils: clay-limestone soil on top of the hills, more clayey soils in the lower slopes and, here and there, some gravelly zones. In addition, they are all characterized by a south or southeast exposure. The red wines of Côtes de Bordeaux are primarily made from merlot, followed by cabernet sauvignon and cabernet franc. Carmenère, malbec (or côt) and petit verdot may also be used in smaller quantities.

Because of their wide variety of terroirs, the wines of Côtes de Bourg have a personality that changes from one estate to the other; the emphasis being, depending on the case, either on tannic strength or on aromatic power. They have a silky mouthfeel and can be enjoyed young, but they can also age for a decade in the cellar. These wines are for people who love fruit. Sainte-Foy-Bordeaux and Graves de Vayres wines are soft and fruity, round and fleshy with a solid tannic structure. They have good aging potential. The appellation Graves de Vayres (not to be confused with the Graves appellation) gets its name from its soil, made of alluvial gravel. The wines of Blaye-Côtes de Bordeaux, which are produced on the right bank of the Gironde, are generally smooth, delicate, fruity and pleasant. As they age, they develop a brick-red color and spicy, musky fragrances, depending on the grape varieties they are based on. The red wines of Cadillac-Côtes de Bordeaux are remarkable for their dense color and strong body, while also being delicate and aromatic. In the small —but hearty— appellation Francs-Côtes de Bordeaux, wines are opulent, full-bodied and generous, but not devoid of finesse, like their neighbors in the Castillon-Côtes de Bordeaux appellation, to which they are significantly similar by intensity and concentration.

2

THE EIGHT AOCs IN THE CÔTES APPELLATION GROUP (REDS)

Blaye-Côtes de Bordeaux, Cadillac-Côtes de Bordeaux, Castillon-Côtes de Bordeaux, Francs-Côtes de Bordeaux, Côtes de Bordeaux, Côtes de Bourg, Graves de Vayres, Sainte-Foy-Bordeaux.

BORDEAUX

CÔTES DE BORDEAUX

1 - BOURG & CÔTES DE BOURG
2 - BLAYE & BLAYE-CÔTES DE BORDEAUX
3 - CADILLAC-CÔTES DE BORDEAUX
4 - CASTILLON-CÔTES DE BORDEAUX
5 - FRANCS-CÔTES DE BORDEAUX
6 - GRAVES DE VAYRES
7 - SAINTE-FOY-BORDEAUX

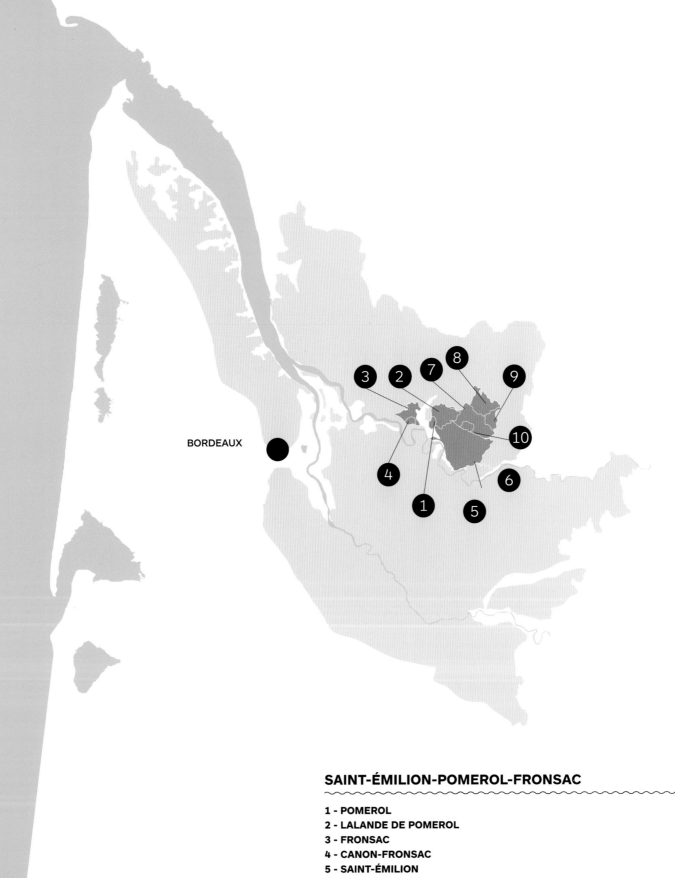

BORDEAUX

SAINT-ÉMILION-POMEROL-FRONSAC

1 - POMEROL
2 - LALANDE DE POMEROL
3 - FRONSAC
4 - CANON-FRONSAC
5 - SAINT-ÉMILION
6 - SAINT-ÉMILION GRAND CRU
7 - MONTAGNE-SAINT-ÉMILION
8 - LUSSAC-SAINT-ÉMILION
9 - PUISSEGUIN-SAINT-ÉMILION
10 - SAINT-GEORGES-SAINT-ÉMILION

3

SAINT-ÉMILION-POMEROL-FRONSAC (REDS)

This area is located on the right bank of the Dordogne, around the city of Libourne. It is a red wine vineyard where merlot dominates. Indeed, in this region, the highly varied soils often contain clay (clay-limestone soils, sandy clay, clay and gravel) and are favorable to the full expression of this variety's organoleptic qualities, completed by cabernet franc. Thus they are generally long-keeping wines that combine smoothness, power and nobility with delicate, subtle flavors. The vineyard of this region offers landscapes of great diversity. From the South, the medieval town of Saint-Émilion, a Unesco World Heritage landmark, can be seen from many miles away, perched on the scalloped edges of a limestone plateau. From the West, just out of Libourne, lies an ocean of vines, dotted with beautiful mansions and small groves. Everywhere, along the winding roads, superb views may be enjoyed from hilltops, plateaus and cliffs over the silver ribbon of the Dordogne river, large valleys carpeted with vineyards, the steeple of Saint-Émilion surrounded by its steep, labyrinthine streets. "The hill of a thousand castles", an expression commonly used to describe this region, only reflects the fact that all the vine plots form a true mosaic, a configuration that dates back to late medieval land and economic patterns. It is also a reminder that the Saint-Émilion and Saint-Émilion Grand Cru appellation officially include over 800 wine growers. Saint-Émilion is not only a famous wine appellation; it is also a world-famous ancient fortified village attracting many tourists, and a Unesco World Heritage destination that greets more than one million visitors each year. Since 1954, Saint-Émilion's great wines have been classified by the INAO, a classification that is revised every ten years. The wines produced in the geographical area of the Saint-Émilion appellation can appear under two appellations: Saint-Émilion and Saint-Émilion Grand Cru. In the latter category, the wines can be designated by the mentions "Grand Cru classé" or "Premier Grand Cru classé." Both Saint-Émilion and Saint-Émilion Grand Cru, as well as their satellites appellations, have a very wide range of soils and subsoils due to erosion: thus one may find asteriated limestone, sandy-gravelly hills, clay-limestone with sandstone, or sandy brown soil on a layer of clay: delicate wines with a rich bouquet stand alongside more full-bodied wines with smooth and generous tannins. These are extremely varied wines, alternately offering softness, power, finesse, fruit and minerality.

THE TEN AOCs OF SAINT-ÉMILION-POMEROL-FRONSAC

Saint-Émilion, Saint-Émilion Grand Cru, Lussac-Saint-Émilion, Saint-Georges-Saint-Émilion, Montagne-Saint-Émilion, Puisseguin-Saint-Émilion. West of Libourne: Fronsac, Canon-Fronsac, Lalande-de-Pomerol and Pomerol.

The vineyard of Pomerol was created in the 12th century by the Knights Hospitallers of St. John of Jerusalem, who grew vines for the Church and for pilgrims on their way to Santiago de Compostela. The mostly clayey soils appear in many different forms depending on the place (including a famous layer of iron oxide) and provide many styles of wines: soft and smooth; or fresh and heady, with notes of licorice; or complex and dense with dense tannins; or round, velvety and fleshy. The wines of Pomerol have never been classified in the way that their Médoc, Graves and Saint-Émilion counterparts have been, but they include very fine wines, including the prestigious Petrus. The wines of Lalande-de-Pomerol are generally colorful, fragrant and rich in very round tannins. The landscape of Fronsac (Fronsac and Canon-Fronsac), radically different from those of Saint-Émilion and Pomerol, was in the time of Louis XIV — who greatly enjoyed its wines for their exceptional quality — one of the most coveted in the region. Everyone wanted to plant grapes in this rich and generous terroir. Fronsac wines are complex and expressive, with powerful and fleshy tannins that can be tight while the wine is very young, but they give it a good aging potential.

MÉDOC AND GRAVES (REDS)

The region of Médoc and Graves covers slightly over 20,000 hectares on the left bank of the Garonne and of the Dordogne. The 45th North parallel runs right through the middle of the Médoc vineyard, which is wedged between the Atlantic ocean and the Gironde estuary. Further to the south, the vineyard of Graves is located between the ocean and the Garonne. Owing to their geographical situation, both these vineyards enjoy a temperate oceanic climate, an excellent condition for the development of the vine. The region benefits from a regular amount of sunshine and of moderate sea breezes, filtered and slowed down by the Landes pine forest. Médoc, with its 16,029 hectares of vine-planted surface, represents 14% of the Bordeaux vineyard. Both small and large wine properties are found here, with small estates (5 to 15 hectares) making up 15% of Médoc properties, and the large estates (30 to 80 hectares) more than 20%. The entire Médoc vineyard is tended and exploited by about one thousand wine growers. The peninsula includes six communal appellations (at the level of the *commune*, or municipality in the French administrative system) and two regional appellations (see boxed text).

The region of Graves, covering 2,505 hectares, represents 2% of the Bordeaux vineyard. It begins just north of the city of Bordeaux, at the Jalle de Blanquefort (a *jalle* is a small stream that runs eastward through the Médoc across its vertical axis, towards the Gironde) and ends just past Langon, upstream alongside the Garonne to the south of the city. There, too, the vast Landes pine forest acts as a border and as a protection against ocean winds. More than 300 wine growers take care of the vines in which two appellations may issue either red or white wines: Graves and Pessac-Léognan.

Cabernet sauvignon, associated with merlot, is heavily used in Médoc blends, generally as the dominant variety, giving them the full benefit of its strong personality. Merlot follows as the secondary grape, and petit verdot is often present in moderate quantity, as a "blending booster", bringing a deep color, notes of black fruits and violet, and a robust tannic framework. Médoc wines are endowed with generous aromas, a harmonious balance, and plenty of body and structure. Their tannins are astringent in youth, then gain delicacy and finesse after some years. They are long-aging wines.

The Médoc appellation covers 35% of the Bordeaux vineyard. Its area includes all the wine-producing villages north of Bordeaux, on the left bank of the Garonne. The appellation, characterized by a great number of small wine properties, produces strong-bodied, structured, generous wines that offer a sensation of fullness upon tasting. They have a beautiful aromatic range, with pleasant notes of licorice, red fruit and black fruit.

A long, 60-kilometer-wide corridor, the Haut-Médoc winds its way among the communal appellations, running through more than twenty *communes*. Consisting mostly of Garonne gravel, this region is particularly known for the variety of its soils, which explain the amazing differences in styles between the wines of the AOC. Haut-Médoc wines are aromatically complex, revealing lovely aromas of red fruit, black fruit, and licorice, with the odd mentholated or spicy note.

Moulis, covering over 7 kilometers from East to West, is the smallest Médoc AOC, but it includes a concentration of exceptional terroirs. Its wines are balanced and elegant, sometimes very full-bodied, but always round and pleasantly smooth. They have exceptional aging abilities.

The Listrac AOC, proudly peaking at 43 meters of altitude, is also known as the "roof of the Médoc". Sheltered from the ocean winds by the pine forest, its vineyard is set upon three gravelly terraces resting on a limestone subsoil. Its dense, deep-colored wines exhale fragrances of red fruit and black fruit, licorice, sweet spices or leather. In the mouth, they are swift and frank. They are balanced, nicely structured, richly aromatic wines.

The Margaux AOC covers five communes: Margaux, Soussans, Arsac, Labarde and Cantenac. It produces wines of every level of the 1855 classification, from the First Growth to the Fifth, as well as Crus Bourgeois and Crus Artisans. Its soils, mostly gravelly and organized in clusters of *croupes* (soft-sloped hills) polished by erosion, slowly dropping towards the river. The wines are characterized by exceptional finesse, a suave, delicate and complex bouquet, and flowery, spicy, sometimes toasty aromas.

The terroir of Saint-Julien is distinguished by the good quality of its soils of well-drained Garonne gravels, and the wines of this appellation are remarkable for the density of their admirable garnet and ruby colors. Their aromatic palette is intense and complex, with notes of blueberry, blackcurrant, blackberry, prune, tobacco, and licorice. Aging adds pleasant aromas of leather, animal fur or truffle. The mouth is dense and opulent, with powerful, smooth tannins.

The territory of the Pauillac AOC is instantly recognizable from its rolling *croupes* of Garonne gravel, imparting to the landscape a unique look and exceptional wine-growing qualities. Pauillac wines are rich, dense, profound, and elegant. Their extremely wide aromatic palette includes black cherry, licorice, crème de

THE TEN AOCs OF MÉDOC AND GRAVES

Médoc: Margaux, Moulis, Listrac-Médoc, Saint-Julien, Pauillac, Saint-Estèphe (appellations communales), Médoc et Haut-Médoc (appellations régionales).
Graves: Graves, Pessac-Léognan.

BORDEAUX

MÉDOC AND GRAVES

1 - MÉDOC
2 - HAUT-MÉDOC
3 - LISTRAC-MÉDOC
4 - MOULIS-EN-MÉDOC
5 - MARGAUX
6 - PAUILLAC
7 - SAINT-ESTÈPHE
8 - SAINT-JULIEN
9 - GRAVES
10 - PESSAC-LÉOGNAN

cassis, sour cherry, rose, cedarwood, smoky notes, etc. The tannins are tight without being harsh. They are generally quite full-bodied and should be fully enjoyed after a few years of aging. Eighteen Classified Growths (Grands Crus classés) are included in the appellation, and among them three First growths (out of five). The Classified Growths represent 85% of the production of Pauillac.

Halfway between Bordeaux and the Pointe de Grave, Saint-Estèphe is characterized by a large geological variety of soils and subsoils and a distinctly hilly relief of well-drained croupes. The wines are enchanting with a beautiful aromatic palette which harmoniously combines red fruits, black fruits, mocha, or vanilla... They are rich, fruity, always well structured, with a great ability to improve over time, while still being pleasant in their youth.

The Graves AOC is spread out on the left bank of the Garonne, south of Bordeaux, on a stretch of 50 kilometers. The terroir, rich in quaternary gravel on a sandy substrate, has a perfect microclimate for wine growing. The red wines of Graves, when young, develop aromas of red fruits with spicy and toasty notes. They are elegant and structured as well as delicate and aromatic, and they age harmoniously. Depending on the vintage and châteaux, they reach their peak between five and ten years of age.

On the southern boundary of the city of Bordeaux, Pessac-Léognan was probably the exact starting point of wine growing in Bordeaux two thousand years ago. The soils of the appellation are made of a thick layer of gravel on a substrate of sand, hardpan (a sort of sandstone solidified by ferrous cement) and clay in varying proportions. All the classified growths of Graves are gathered together in the Pessac-Léognan appellation. Because of their location right outside of the city of Bordeaux, the vineyard of this appellation struggles daily to protect its high-value wine terroirs from urban development. The wines have a deep, intense color. In the mouth, they are dense and fleshy. In middle age appears an excellent bouquet where scents of leather mix with wood, prune and truffle. These wines can age for many years.

TERRES DE GRAVES

Not everyone agrees about the etymology of the name Médoc: some identify it as a Gascon word for "middle earth", others evoke a Latin root meaning "in the midst of the waters." It cannot be denied that this long peninsular strip extends between the Atlantic Ocean and the Gironde estuary, known locally as "the River". It is sandy, with woodlands to the West (Landes du Médoc) and, further east, near the Gironde, poor, pebbly soils of Pyrenean gravel carried by the Garonne in the Tertiary and early Quaternary eras, as well as Dordogne gravel brought later from the Massif Central.

These Médoc lands were long neglected because of their gravelly soil on which nothing seemed to grow. And little wine was made there until merchants noticed, following the invention of the New French Claret with its more structured body and better aging ability, that these unloved soils were particularly favorable to the vine plant. From this point, in the 18th century, a vast red-wine vineyard flourished in the Médoc, mostly planted in cabernet sauvignon, a late variety that prefers warm, well-drained soils. As a matter of fact, these gravelly soils have the ability not only to reflect solar heat during the day, but also to absorb some that they radiate during the night, thereby reducing the daily temperature differences and sometimes even averting night frost.

Bordering the city of Bordeaux, in the southeastern extension of the Médoc, Graves wines are the only ones in France to be named after their soil: *las Grabas de Bourdeus*, literally "Bordeaux gravels". The vineyard of Graves rests on soils that are similar to those of the Médoc, but the thickness of their gravel layer is more uneven, mixed with sand, clay or limestone. The red wines of northern Graves (the Pessac-Léognan AOC, created in 1987) are strong and robust, with deep color and considerable aging power. The AOC includes all the great classified growths of the area. The red wines of southern Graves are lighter but well-balanced, with delicate aromas.

The red wines of Graves, when young, develop aromas of red fruits with spicy and toasty notes.

BORDEAUX DRY WHITES

Sémillon represents 55% of the plantings for dry white wines and remains the dominant white variety for Bordeaux wines. Its good aging qualities are particularly evident in the great, barrel-aged dry whites (Graves and Pessac-Léognan). Sémillon's qualities make it complementary to Sauvignon. It brings roundness and a floral touch to blends.

Sauvignon is the white grape that has increased the most in recent years, making up 34% of the plantings in white. It is particularly tasty, round and lively at the same time, with a wide range of aromas: citrus, tropical fruits, blackcurrant bud, boxwood or white flowers. When its yields are controlled and the grape has sufficient strength and richness, it produces deep, powerful, complex white wines that may be aged in oak barrels.

Muscadelle is not widely planted because it is a demanding variety and not easy to grow, with sometimes erratic results, but it has floral aromas reminiscent of muscat. In blends, it brings roundness to livelier and more acidic sauvignon wines.

The Bordeaux Blanc sec (dry white) AOC may be produced throughout the wine growing zone of the department of the Gironde. These wines are pale yellow in color with more or less of a golden hue. They develop elegant flavors of citrus and white fruits, accompanied by floral notes of boxwood, broom or acacia blossoms, sometimes associated with toasty or buttery aromas from barrel aging.

The Entre-Deux-Mers AOC, located between the Dordogne and the Garonne, owes its name to the fact that these two rivers, under the influence of ocean tides, behave like inland seas. Dating back to Gallo-Roman times, this vineyard was later developed by Benedictine monks. These are aromatic white wines with a palette of citrus, yellow flowers and tropical fruits. In the mouth, they are lively, generous and smooth, with a refreshing acidity.

The dry white wines of Graves are based on sémillon and sauvignon. White Graves have a complex and intense nose with aromas of citrus, passion fruit, flowers (broom, acacia...), boxwood or even dried fruit. In the mouth, they show vivacity, roundness and generosity, with a lot of freshness. The white Pessac-Léognan (from a subregion of Graves) usually contain more sauvignon that Graves. They are stylish, elegant and powerful with aromas of boxwood, hawthorn, citrus and blackcurrant bud. In the mouth, they are complex with a good balance of vivacity, fruit, roundness, power, and great aromatic persistence. The best of them are adapted to a lengthy aging in oak barrels.

The sharp, fresh dry white wines of the Blaye-Côtes de Bordeaux appellation display some delicious lemony notes. They are based on a blend of Sauvignon and Sémillon. Auxiliary varieties like colombard and ugni blanc bring freshness and liveliness. The dry whites produced in the Graves de Vayres, Côtes de Bourg and Francs-Côtes de Bordeaux appellations are vinified with utmost care due to their limited production. Based on sauvignon, sémillon, muscadelle and sometimes colombard, they are fermented in vats or in barrels. The soils in these areas are mostly clay-limestone.

THE TWELVE AOCs OF BORDEAUX BLANC SEC

Bordeaux blanc, Bordeaux-Haut-Benauge, Entre-Deux-Mers, Entre-Deux-Mers-Haut-Benauge, Blaye-Côtes de Bordeaux, Côtes de Bourg, Francs-Côtes de Bordeaux, Graves, Pessac-Léognan, Graves de Vayres, Sainte-Foy-Bordeaux and Crémant de Bordeaux.

BORDEAUX

THE DRY WHITE WINES

1 - CÔTES DE BLAYE
2 - BLAYE-CÔTES DE BORDEAUX
3 - BOURG
4 - CÔTES DE BOURG
5 - FRANCS-CÔTES DE BORDEAUX
6 - CÔTES DE BORDEAUX-SAINT-MACAIRE
7 - GRAVES DE VAYRES
8 - SAINTE-FOY-BORDEAUX
9 - ENTRE-DEUX-MERS
10 - ENTRE-DEUX-MERS-HAUT-BENAUGE
11 - GRAVES
12 - PESSAC-LÉOGNAN

BORDEAUX DRY WHITE & CRÉMANT DE BORDEAUX (WHITE): AOCs PRODUCED ACROSS THE ENTIRE BORDEAUX VINEYARD AREA

BORDEAUX

MOELLEUX (SEMI-SWEET) WHITE WINES

1 - CÔTES DE BORDEAUX-SAINT-MACAIRE
2 - GRAVES SUPÉRIEURES
3 - PREMIÈRES CÔTES DE BORDEAUX
4 - SAINTE-FOY-BORDEAUX

LIQUOREUX (SWEET) WHITE WINES

5 - BARSAC
6 - CADILLAC
7 - CÉRONS
8 - LOUPIAC
9 - SAINTE-CROIX-DU-MONT
10 - SAUTERNES

BORDEAUX SUPÉRIEUR: AOC PRODUCED ACROSS THE ENTIRE BORDEAUX VINEYARD AREA

SWEET BORDEAUX (MOELLEUX AND LIQUOREUX)

These wines are mostly based on sémillon (around 80%), sauvignon (about 20 %) and a minor proportion of muscadelle for aromatic reasons. They can be produced on many different types of soils: clayey, flinty, gravelly, or limestone on the left bank of the Garonne, and clayey limestone, clayey gravel or clayey sand on the right bank. As a whole, the eleven Sweet Bordeaux appellations represent 3,517 hectares of producing vineyards, which is barely 3% of the entire Bordeaux production. They are exceptional, rare wines. They are all the more precious because their yield is very low. In Bordeaux, it is said that one vine plant produces one bottle of red or dry white wine, but only one glass of liquoreux wine.

MOELLEUX WINES

Moelleux from the Premières Côtes de Bordeaux are fresh and lively, offering notes of acacia blossoms, vanilla or peach. Warm and mellow, they may be drunk young or after a few years of aging. Those of the Francs-Côtes de Bordeaux appellation often display exuberant tropical fruit aromas. Graves Supérieures are dense, round and subtle moelleux white wines with notes of citrus, peach, acacia blossom and honey. Moelleux wines of the Bordeaux Supérieur appellation may be produced in all the wine growing communes of the Bordelais and on all types of soils, but they cover no more than fifty hectares. They are fruity, smooth, and lively. In the eastern part of the department, the Sainte-Foy-Bordeaux appellation mostly produces red wines, but it also makes a small amount of light, delicate and fruity moelleux wines. Finally, the Côtes-de-Bordeaux Saint-Macaire region makes smooth, lively moelleux whites.

WHAT IS THE DIFFERENCE BETWEEN MOELLEUX AND LIQUOREUX?

It is important, within the Sweet Bordeaux appellation, to distinguish the moelleux from the liquoreux. All Sweet Bordeaux are white wines that are obtained from late, prolonged harvests, and undergo an incomplete fermentation. Through the action of noble rot, a certain proportion of the natural grape sugar fails to be converted into alcohol. This amount is called "residual sugar", and its degree is decisive in the classification of a wine into the moelleux or the liquoreux category (see text to the right and page 68). If the amount of residual sugar stands between 4 and 45 g per liter, it is a moelleux. If the amount of residual sugar exceeds 45 g per liter, then it is a liquoreux.

THE ELEVEN AOCs OF SWEET BORDEAUX

Five appellations produce moelleux white wines: Bordeaux Supérieur, Sainte-Foy-Bordeaux, Côtes de Bordeaux-Saint-Macaire, Premières Côtes de Bordeaux, Graves Supérieures. Six appellations produce liquoreux white wines: Sauternes, Barsac, Cérons, Cadillac, Loupiac, and Sainte-Croix-du-Mont.

LIQUOREUX WINES

The liquoreux white wines of the Sauternais are a gift of local hygrometry. This region, which includes the three appellations Sauternes, Barsac and Cérons, enjoys a very special microclimate produced by a small stream, the Ciron, which weaves its way on the left bank of the Garonne and creates the mandatory conditions for creating great liquoreux wines. The daily succession of humidity and dryness that dominates in the air when the grapes have reached their full maturity favors the development of *Botrytis cinerea*, a microscopic fungus also called noble rot (*pourriture noble*). This very common fungus is dreaded in other wine regions, for it ruins the grapes, and is known in that case as "grey rot" (*pourriture grise*). In the particular case of liquoreux wines, it attacks the grape berries differently. First, it penetrates into the berry and invades it, coating the inside of the skin with mycelium, thus giving it a brownish purple color. This stage it is called "full rot" (*pourri plein*). In order to develop, *Botrytis cinerea* eats some of the sugar and acids contained in the berry's juice. Then, through the effect of pectolitic enzymes, it degrades the berry's skin significantly, making it highly permeable. The water quickly evaporates from the grape's juice, causing the berry to wither and the main components of the juice to concentrate. This is the *pourri rôti* ("roasted rot") stage. Besides this, the interactions between the fungus and the vine plant trigger chemical reactions that produce considerable aromatic amplification. This evolution in quality is a rather slow process and does not develop evenly on all grape clusters. That is the reason why the harvest is performed in several *tries*, or stages, harvesters picking only the botrytized clusters or parts of clusters at each successive trie. From this subtle alchemy, the great Bordeaux liquoreux wines are born. In their youth, they are ample, fruity, and energetic. Throughout the years, these extremely long-keeping wines develop plenty of smoothness, a fantastic bouquet and their unmistakable elegance.

The geographical area of the Sauternes appellation, about forty kilometers southeast of Bordeaux, includes five communes: Sauternes, Fargues, Bommes, Preignac and Barsac. Of these five, only Barsac is allowed to print either "Barsac" or "Barsac-Sauternes" on its labels. The soil of Sauternes is hugely varied, resulting in many different wine typicalities: clay, sand and gravel are stacked into distinct layers, forming gently rolling hills or *croupes*. The wines of Sauternes have the color of old gold and can age for many years. Their evoke citrus, acacia, and apricot in a complex balance. In the mouth, they have sweetness, roundness, power and exceptional "roasted" character. The 1855 classification distinguished ten Sauternes growths, with Château d'Yquem

HOW LIQUOREUX WINES WERE BORN

There is something very striking in the sight of a botrytized cluster of grapes — all brown and shriveled, literally covered with fluff, it does not look inviting to taste. Yet, from their juice, a divine nectar is produced. It is hard to believe that before a liquoreux wine could exist, someone had to imagine the possibility that under that layer of rot, called "noble" in this exclusive case, such a wine could be produced.

It seems that late harvesting was already practiced in the 16th century. In the 17th century, Dutch traders, while great lovers of sweet wines, were not willing to pay the price of the lengthy harvests by successive selections that characterizes liquoreux wines. At the time, semi-liquoreux wines were produced in the Prévôté of Barsac, the territory of the present Barsac-Sauternes appellation. It seems that the production of true liquoreux became widespread in the 18th century, thanks to the interest of passionate amateurs like Thomas Jefferson or the Grand Duke Constantine of Russia, which encouraged wine growers to sort the grapes more carefully for a better selection of the noble rot. From the last quarter of the 18th century, Sauternes châteaux sought to promote the quality of their wines and the practice of tries was generalized. However, the great era of liquoreux did not start before the first half of the 19th century.

as the only Premier Cru Supérieur (First Superior Growth).

The wines of the commune of Barsac, 38 kilometers southeast of Bordeaux, at the mouth of Ciron, may be labeled as Barsac or Sauternes. The terroir of Barsac is a low-lying plateau which comprises three main types of soil: alluvial deposits near the Garonne, Garonne gravel, and finally the zone called "Plateau de Barsac", clay-limestone on a limestone subsoil. The wines have a deep, aromatic nose, both delicate and elegant, and an ample, fresh and lengthy mouthfeel. Ten classified growths were selected by the 1855 classification on the commune of Barsac.

The Cérons appellation is located 35 kilometers southeast of Bordeaux, on the left bank of the Garonne. It can be claimed by three communes — Illats, Cérons and Podensac. The siliceous gravelly soil is in some places clayey-gravelly, or even sandy. The subsoil is mostly limestone. The wines of the appellation Cérons have a highly developed bouquet; they are complex, delicate, generous and fruity.

At nearly 40 kilometers southeast of Bordeaux, on the right bank of the Garonne, the hills of Loupiac produce sweet wine that can age a very long time, very soft with a delicate fruitiness. Five kilometers upstream, the vineyards of Sainte-Croix-du-Mont covers hillsides that are often quite steep. The terroir is mainly composed of clay-limestone soils in which clumps of oyster shells and other varieties of marine fossils sometimes appear. The wines of Sainte-Croix-du-Mont are fruity, concentrated and elegant, eagerly waiting to improve over the years. These two appellations can be made only in their respective communes.

The Cadillac appellation is named after a city on the right bank of the Garonne, also about forty kilometers southeast of Bordeaux. It can be claimed by twenty-two villages. The landscape is hilly, sometimes steep. Depending on the sector, clay-limestone soils or gravel cover a limestone or clay-limestone subsoil. The wines of Cadillac are elegant, aromatic, fruity and concentrated.

GRANDS CRUS
AND *CLASSIFICATIONS*

The wines of Bordeaux owe much of their worldwide reputation to their great classified growths (Grands Crus classés), eminent symbols of quality and prestige. Indeed, the concept of classification was created in Bordeaux through the 1855 classification, a list gathering the most prestigious wines of Médoc and Sauternes based on the observation of their commercial success.

CLASSIFIED GROWTHS

A cru is the synthesis of nature and the work of man — on one hand, it can only be produced on terroirs with a poor, well-drained soil, into which the roots of the vine plant may dive deeply to find the nutrients they lack on the surface, thus capturing the mineral wealth of the earth. On the other hand, it also reflects the efforts of men who followed each other through generations, devoting themselves to quality. Bordeaux *grands crus* appeared long before they were classified: Château Haut-Brion appeared in 1609, followed by Château Margaux in 1703, then by Château Lafite and Château Latour. From then on, the number of these *grands crus* increased and their quality was asserted. They are now identified in four wine regions: Médoc, Graves, Saint-Émilion and Sauternes-Barsac. It should be pointed out that not being classified does not prevent an appellation — like Pomerol — or a wine — such as Petrus — to be considered first-rate.

THE 1855 CLASSIFICATION (MÉDOC AND SAUTERNES)

On the occasion of the 1855 Universal Exposition in Paris, Emperor Napoleon III asked each wine region of France that showcased their wines to establish a ranking of them. For the Gironde, the task was entrusted to the Bordeaux Chamber of Commerce and Industry of Bordeaux, founded in 1705. The Bordeaux CCI in turn asked the Union of wine brokers at the Bordeaux stock exchange to compile the classification of red wines and white wines of the Gironde. Only the red wines of Médoc, the sweet white wines of Sauternes and Barsac, and one red growth of Graves are represented in that list. The reason for this could be the absence of a Chamber of Commerce and Industry in Libourne at the time — it was not created until 1910 — and the dominant position of the wines sold by the city of Bordeaux's traders. The classification was based on the reputation of the wines and on their transaction prices, and it was revised only once since 1855, in 1973, and only for one Médoc wine, following a contest organized by the Bordeaux Chamber of Commerce. The only change was the reclassification of Château Mouton Rothschild, hitherto a Second Growth, to the rank of First Growth. Sixty classified growths of the Médoc make up about 24% of the total wine production in the peninsula. It is important to point out that for a given growth, only the grand vin made by the château is classified.

For more information, see the official website of the Conseil des Grands Crus classés en 1855
www.crus-classes.com

THE CLASSIFICATIONS OF THE BORDEAUX VINEYARD

There are several classifications in the Gironde:
• The 1855 classification, gathering growths from Médoc (reds), Sauternes (liquoreux whites), and one growth from Graves (red).
• The Graves classification (reds and whites, first established in 1953).
• The Saint-Émilion classification (reds, first established in 1954).
• The classification of Crus bourgeois de Médoc (reds, first established in 1932).
• The classification of Crus artisans (reds, first established in 2002).

The great classified growths are identified in four regions: Médoc, Graves, Saint-Émilion and Sauternes-Barsac.

Regarding red wines, the 1855 classification, revised in 1973, includes one growth of Graves and sixty growths of Médoc, thus listed:

FIRST CLASSIFIED GROWTHS

Château Haut-Brion, Pessac, Pessac-Léognan AOC

Château Lafite-Rothschild, Pauillac, Pauillac AOC

Château Latour, Pauillac, Pauillac AOC

Château Margaux, Margaux, Margaux AOC

Château Mouton Rothschild, Pauillac, Pauillac AOC

SECOND CLASSIFIED GROWTHS

Château Brane-Cantenac, Cantenac, Margaux AOC

Château Cos-d'Estournel, Saint-Estèphe, Saint-Estèphe AOC

Château Ducru-Beaucaillou, Saint-Julien-Beychevelle, Saint-Julien AOC

Château Durfort-Vivens, Margaux, Margaux AOC

Château Gruaud-Larose, Saint-Julien-Beychevelle, Saint-Julien AOC

Château Lascombes, Margaux, Margaux AOC

Château Léoville-Barton, Saint-Julien-Beychevelle, Saint-Julien AOC

Château Léoville-Las-Cases, Saint-Julien-Beychevelle, Saint-Julien AOC

Château Léoville-Poyferré, Saint-Julien-Beychevelle, Saint-Julien AOC

Château Montrose, Saint-Estèphe, Saint-Estèphe AOC

Château Pichon-Longueville-Baron-de-Pichon, Pauillac, Pauillac AOC

Château Pichon-Longueville-Comtesse-de-Lalande, Pauillac, Pauillac AOC

Château Rauzan-Ségla, Margaux, Margaux AOC

Château Rauzan-Gassies, Margaux, Margaux AOC

THIRD CLASSIFIED GROWTHS

Château Boyd-Cantenac, Cantenac, Margaux AOC

Château Calon-Ségur, Saint-Estèphe, Saint-Estèphe AOC

Château Cantenac-Brown, Cantenac, Margaux AOC

Château Desmirail, Margaux, Margaux AOC

Château Ferrière, Margaux, Margaux AOC

Château Giscours, Labarde, Margaux AOC

Château d'Issan, Cantenac, Margaux AOC

Château Kirwan, Cantenac, Margaux AOC

Château Lagrange, Saint-Julien-Beychevelle, Saint-Julien AOC

Château La Lagune, Ludon, Haut-Médoc AOC

Château Langoa-Barton, Saint-Julien-Beychevelle, Saint-Julien AOC

Château Malescot-Saint-Exupéry, Margaux, Margaux AOC

Château Marquis-d'Alesme, Margaux, Margaux AOC

Château Palmer, Cantenac, Margaux AOC

FOURTH CLASSIFIED GROWTHS

Château Beychevelle, Saint-Julien-Beychevelle, Saint-Julien AOC

Château Branaire-Ducru, Saint-Julien-Beychevelle, Saint-Julien AOC

Château Duhart-Milon, Pauillac, Pauillac AOC

Château Lafon-Rochet, Saint-Estèphe, Saint-Estèphe AOC

Château Marquis-de-Terme, Margaux, Margaux AOC

Château Pouget, Cantenac, Margaux AOC

Château Prieuré-Lichine, Cantenac, Margaux AOC

Château Saint-Pierre, Saint-Julien-Beychevelle, Saint-Julien AOC

Château Talbot, Saint-Julien-Beychevelle, Saint-Julien AOC

Château La Tour-Carnet, Saint-Laurent-de-Médoc, Haut-Médoc AOC

FIFTH CLASSIFIED GROWTHS

Château d'Armailhac, Pauillac, Pauillac AOC

Château Batailley, Pauillac, Pauillac AOC

Château Belgrave, Saint-Laurent-de-Médoc, Haut-Médoc AOC

Château Camensac, Saint-Laurent-de-Médoc, Haut-Médoc AOC

Château Cantemerle, Macau, Haut-Médoc AOC

Château Clerc-Milon, Pauillac, Pauillac AOC

Château Cos-Labory, Saint-Estèphe, Saint-Estèphe AOC

Château Croizet-Bages, Pauillac, Pauillac AOC

Château Dauzac, Labarde, Margaux AOC

Château Grand-Puy-Ducasse, Pauillac, Pauillac AOC

Château Grand-Puy-Lacoste, Pauillac, Pauillac AOC

Château Haut-Bages-Libéral, Pauillac, Pauillac AOC

Château Haut-Batailley, Pauillac, Pauillac AOC

Château Lynch-Bages, Pauillac, Pauillac AOC

Château Lynch-Moussas, Pauillac, Pauillac AOC

Château Pédesclaux, Pauillac, Pauillac AOC

Château Pontet-Canet, Pauillac, Pauillac AOC

Château du Tertre, Arsac, Margaux AOC

Regarding the liquoreux white wines, the 1855 classification includes twenty-six growths of Sauternes et Barsac, thus listed:

FIRST SUPERIOR CLASSIFIED GROWTH

Château d'Yquem, Sauternes, Sauternes AOC

FIRST CLASSIFIED GROWTHS

Château Climens, Barsac, Barsac AOC

Clos Haut-Peyraguey, Bommes, Sauternes AOC

Château Coutet, Barsac, Barsac AOC

Château Guiraud, Sauternes, Sauternes AOC

Château Lafaurie-Peyraguey, Bommes, Sauternes AOC

Château Rabaud-Promis, Bommes, Sauternes AOC

Château Rayne-Vigneau, Bommes, Sauternes AOC

Château Rieussec, Fargues-de-Langon, Sauternes AOC

Château Sigalas-Rabaud, Bommes, Sauternes AOC

Château Suduiraut, Preignac, Sauternes AOC

Château La Tour-Blanche, Bommes, Sauternes AOC

SECOND CLASSIFIED GROWTHS

Château d'Arche, Sauternes, Sauternes AOC

Château Broustet, Barsac, Barsac AOC

Château Caillou, Barsac, Barsac AOC

Château Doisy-Daëne, Barsac, Barsac AOC

Château Doisy-Dubroca, Barsac, Barsac AOC

Château Doisy-Védrines, Barsac, Barsac AOC

Château Filhot, Sauternes, Sauternes AOC

Château Lamothe (Despujols), Sauternes, Sauternes AOC

Château Lamothe-Guignard, Sauternes, Sauternes AOC

Château de Malle, Preignac, Sauternes AOC

Château de Myrat, Barsac, Barsac AOC

Château Nairac, Barsac, Barsac AOC

Château Romer-du-Hayot, Fargues-de-Langon, Sauternes AOC

Château Romer, Fargues-de-Langon, Sauternes AOC

Château Suau, Barsac, Barsac AOC

The classified growths of Sauternes and Barsac too are important trade items, since they cover 45% of the surface area of their appellation and represent 30% of its production.

THE GRAVES CLASSIFICATION

In 1953, at the request of the Defense Syndicate of the Graves Appellation to classify that region's great growths, the INAO (National Institute of Protected Geographical Appellations) established a list that was modified and completed later, in 1959. On these terroirs where excellent reds as well as excellent dry whites are produced, the INAO had to classify the growths by communes and types of wine, red or white, resulting in a non-hierarchical classification of 16 growths, all claiming the "Cru classé" mention and belonging to the Pessac-Léognan appellation. It should be noted that there is no mention of a possible revision in the texts.

For more information, see the official website of the Crus classés de Graves: www.crus-classes-de-graves.com

THE CLASSIFIED GROWTHS OF GRAVES

Château Bouscaut, Cadaujac, red and white
Château Carbonnieux, Léognan, red and white
Domaine de-Chevalier, Léognan, red and white
Château Couhins, Villenave-d'Ornon, white
Château Couhins-Lurton, Villenave-d'Ornon, white
Château de Fieuzal, Léognan, red
Château Haut-Bailly, Léognan, red
Château Haut-Brion, Pessac (also a 1855 First Classified Growth), red
Château Latour-Martillac, Martillac, red and white
Château Laville-Haut-Brion, Talence, white
Château Malartic-Lagravière, Léognan, red and white
Château La Mission-Haut-Brion, Talence, red
Château Olivier, Léognan, red and white
Château Pape-Clément, Pessac, red
Château Smith-Haut-Lafite, Martillac, red
Château La Tour-Haut-Brion, Talence, red

THE CLASSIFICATION OF SAINT-ÉMILION

At the request of the Defense Syndicate of the Saint-Émilion appellation, the INAO undertook a classification of the wines of that region as early as 1954. The decree states that the INAO should proceed to the revision of that classification every ten years. Thus, in succession, the following classifications were established:

• First classification in 1954, modified in 1958.

• A second classification was done in 1969.

• The third classification could not be achieved in 1979; it was in 1984 and took effect starting from the 1986 vintage, following the directive of May 23, 1986. It was then stated that any wine produced in the geographical area of the Saint-Émilion appellation could claim either the Saint-Émilion or the Saint-Émilion Grand Cru AOC, but only the wines of the Saint-Émilion Grand Cru could benefit from either the Grand Cru classé or the Premier Grand Cru classé appellation once the official ranking was established.

• The fourth classification, established in 1996, comprised 13 Premiers Grands Crus classés and 55 Grands Crus classés.

• The fifth classification, established in 2006, comprised 15 Premiers Grands Crus classés. This ranking was challenged by some wine growers, which resulted in disputes and in a legal mess. Several times, it was cancelled, reinstated, and then cancelled again, which led the French Senate to cancel it definitely and in its place reinstate the former 1996 classification through an amendment. This was prolongated until 2011, while at the same time authorizing a certain number of properties that had been promoted as Grand Cru classé or Premier Grand Cru classé in the cancelled 2006 ranking to continue displaying these distinctions on their labels. A new classification procedure was scheduled for the 2012 harvest.

• The sixth classification, published on September 6, 2012, is the result of a new procedure that is entirely controlled by the INAO, with the help of the French Ministries of Agriculture and Consumer Affairs. Thus, 82 properties are consecrated — 64 Grands Crus classés and 18 Premiers Grands Crus classés.

For more information, see the official website of the Conseil des vins de Saint-Émilion:
www.vins-saint-emilion.com

THE CLASSIFICATION OF CRUS BOURGEOIS DU MÉDOC

The notion of "Cru Bourgeois" dates back to the Middle Ages, when the *bourgeois* (the affluent families of the *bourg*, or the city, of Bordeaux, although the word originally simply meant "citizen") became richer and acquired the best land in the region. Their properties got their denomination from their owners' social status, their number fluctuating between 200 and 300 châteaux throughout their long history. The Crus Bourgeois were not officially organized into an official list before 1932 by the Bordeaux brokers, under the auspices of the Bordeaux Chamber of Commerce and of the Chamber of Agriculture of the Gironde. The list then included 444 wines. The traditional mention "Cru Bourgeois" was recognized on the labels by communal legislation in 1979. In 2000, the list was hierarchized by merit between Crus Bourgeois Exceptionnels, Crus Bourgeois Supérieurs and Crus Bourgeois. On June 17, 2003, a Ministerial Order finally authorized the first official classification of the Crus Bourgeois, sanctioning 247 châteaux out of 490 applicants. However, in 2007, the Administrative Court of Appeal of Bordeaux cancelled that order. Then the Médoc winemakers, gathered under the Alliance des Crus Bourgeois du Médoc, decide to fight energetically to revive the traditional designation through a rigorous quality policy. In October 2009, the French government approved this new quality approach, which allowed for the annual selection of the Crus Bourgeois du Médoc, whose official list is published each year in September since 2010. Depending on the year, it oscillates between 240 and 260 wine estates. Today, the Crus Bourgeois, all comprised within the eight Médoc AOCs, are still often family-owned châteaux and represent over 40% of the production of the peninsula.

For more information, see the official website of the Crus bourgeois du Médoc:
www.crus-bourgeois.com

THE CRUS ARTISANS DU MÉDOC

In the Médoc, the "Crus artisans" denomination has existed for more than 150 years. It concerns small wine properties originally belonging to Médoc craftspeople — coopers, wheelwrights, blacksmith farriers, etc. Fallen into disuse in the mid-20th century, this distinction was reborn in 1989 with the creation of the Union des Crus Artisans du Médoc, which grouped "autonomous small and medium-sized wine estates whose head owner actually participates in the tending of his vineyard, produces AOC wines, and bottles his products at the château before marketing them". In June 1994, the European regulations reinstated this designation and authorized the printing of the "Cru Artisan" mention on the label. The list was first published at the *Journal officiel* in 2006 then again in 2012, and comprised 44 properties. It is updated every ten years.

For more information, see the official website of the Crus Artisans du Médoc: www.crus-artisans.com

WINE BROTHERHOODS

Bordeaux has thirteen wine societies whose purpose is the promotion of the wines of their appellations. There are also eighty-five Commanderies established worldwide as embassies and enthusiasts of Bordeaux wines. Both brotherhoods and commanderies are under the authority of the Great Council of Bordeaux Wines. Here is the list of Bordeaux wine brotherhoods:
• La Commanderie du Bontemps, bringing together the Confrérie de Médoc et Graves, Sauternes et Barsac, and that of Sainte-Croix-du-Mont
• La Jurade de Saint-Émilion
• Les Hospitaliers de Pomerol (Hospitalers of Pomerol)
• Les Baillis de Lalande-de-Pomerol (Bailliffs of Lalande-de-Pomerol)
• La Connétablie Blaye-Côtes de Bordeaux (Constables of Blaye-Côtes de Bordeaux)
• La Connétablie de Guyenne des Côtes de Bourg (Constables of Guyenne in Côtes de Bourg)
• La Connétablie de Guyenne de l'Entre-Deux-Mers (Constables of Guyenne in Entre-Deux-Mers)
• La Connétablie de Guyenne des Graves de Vayres (Constables of Guyenne in Graves de Vayres)
• La Connétablie de Guyenne en Premières Côtes de Cadillac (Constables of Guyenne in Premières Côtes de Cadillac)
• Les Compagnons du bordeaux (Companions of Bordeaux wine)
• Les Compagnons du Loupiac (Companions of Loupiac wine)
• Les Gentilshommes du duché de Fronsac (Gentlemen of the Duchy of Fronsac)
• L'Ordre des vignerons de Bordeaux et Bordeaux Supérieur (Order of Bordeaux and Bordeaux Supérieur winemakers)

SUMMARY TABLE

GEOGRAPHICAL ZONE	DATE	COLOR(S)	NUMBER OF CHÂTEAUX
MÉDOC (60) AND GRAVES (1)	1855	Red wines	5 First Classified Growths 14 Second Classified Growths 14 Third Classified Growths 10 Fourth Classified Growths 18 Fifth Classified Growths
SAUTERNES AND BARSAC	1855	Liquoreux whites	1 Superior First Classified Growth 11 First Classified Growths 15 Second Classified Growths
GRAVES	1959	Red or white	16 Classified Growths
SAINT-ÉMILION	2012	Red wines	18 First Great Classified Growths 64 Great Classified Growths
CRUS BOURGEOIS	2010	Red wines	260 Crus bourgeois
CRUS ARTISANS	2006	Red wines	13 Médoc AOCs 9 Communal AOCs 22 Haut-Médoc AOCs

3

THE ART
OF BORDEAUX
WINE

THE WINEMAKER'S CALENDAR

From the vineyard to the cellar, each month brings a number of different tasks that will determine the ultimate quality of wine. These tasks are summarized in the following calendar, which begins in October, when the harvest is completed and a new cycle begins in the vineyard.

OCTOBER

During this period, the winemaker carries out the heart of his job — fermenting the grapes into wine. In the vineyard, there is plowing to do following the harvest. During the growing season, the vines have taken all the nutriments they need from the soil need to develop and produce high-quality grapes: now is the perfect time to add some organic fertilizers and minerals to the soil to avoid any deficiency during the next growing season. Plowing also has the effect of covering the base of the vines with soil which protects them from winter frosts: this process is called *chausser* or *cavaillonner* (earthing up).

WINEMAKING CALENDAR

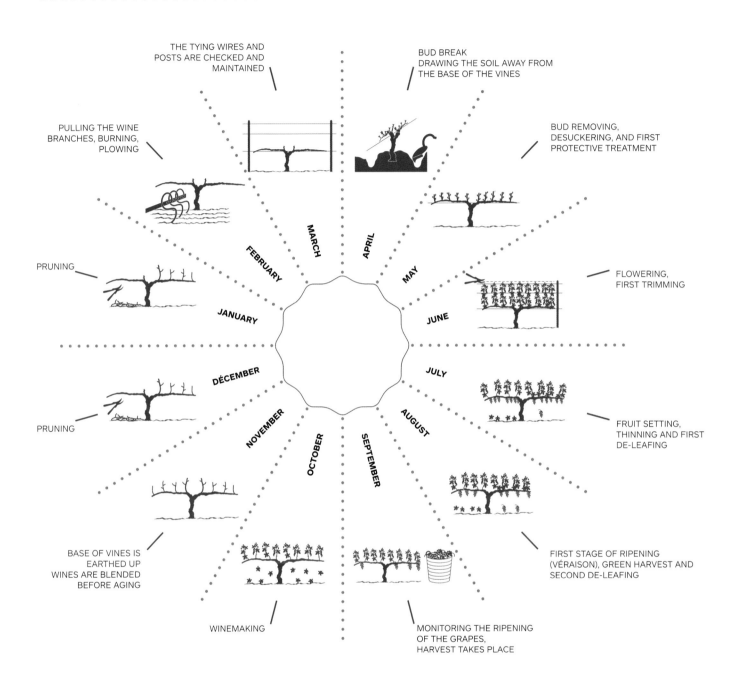

THE TYING WIRES AND POSTS ARE CHECKED AND MAINTAINED

BUD BREAK
DRAWING THE SOIL AWAY FROM THE BASE OF THE VINES

PULLING THE WINE BRANCHES, BURNING, PLOWING

BUD REMOVING, DESUCKERING, AND FIRST PROTECTIVE TREATMENT

PRUNING

FLOWERING, FIRST TRIMMING

PRUNING

FRUIT SETTING, THINNING AND FIRST DE-LEAFING

BASE OF VINES IS EARTHED UP
WINES ARE BLENDED BEFORE AGING

FIRST STAGE OF RIPENING (VÉRAISON), GREEN HARVEST AND SECOND DE-LEAFING

WINEMAKING

MONITORING THE RIPENING OF THE GRAPES, HARVEST TAKES PLACE

MARCH
APRIL
FEBRUARY
MAY
JANUARY
JUNE
DÉCEMBER
JULY
NOVEMBER
AUGUST
OCTOBER
SEPTEMBER

October: grape fermentation is carried out in the cellar while the vineyard is plowed.

NOVEMBER TO JANUARY

Starting from this month, wine growers prepare the vineyard (see pages 93 to 95) by removing the staples and lowering the tying wires to facilitate pruning. Once the vine has shed its leaves, they can proceed with the pruning, which takes place until the middle of March. Pruning is actually the longest and most important task for vine-training, and growers generally start this as early as mid-November, unless they know they can safely complete it within a short period of time.

FEBRUARY

Pruning is followed by removing the cut canes from the vines. Burning and crushing are two different options to eliminate the fallen canes. Mechanical crushing is a faster process, through which the crushed canes left in the rows help to regenerate the soil by an addition of organic matter, while the ashes left from the burning bring minerals to the soil.

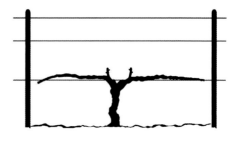

MARCH

Once the plot is pruned and the canes have fallen, the trellising has to be maintained by replacing the posts that have been damaged by weather and machines, fixing any broken wires and tightening the remaining ones. After the trellis system is repaired, the wine grower ties the vine plants to their supports and to the lowest wire. Starting from March, the vine awakes from its long winter sleep and begins a new growth cycle. The sap rises in the shoots and oozes through the scars left by pruning — it is then said that the vine "weeps". From then on, the wine grower must work at the pace of the vine's growth and adapt to the weather conditions.

APRIL

The first stage is characterized by bud break: the buds grow, gradually letting the first leaves and future shoots appear. During this tricky period, the vine grower particularly fears Spring frost, which can harm the crop by burning the young shoot, as was the case in April 1991. This is also the time to remove the earth from the base of the vines to flatten the work surface between rows and under the plants, and to pull out the weeds that grew during Winter. After that is done, the clumps of earth (known as *cavaillons*) between the vine plants have to be removed mechanically. Then the remaining clumps have to be pulled out by hand using a tool called *tire-cavaillon*. This is a tough task, particularly on clay soils that grow hard and compacted after all the rainwater has evaporated.

MAY

Between bud break and flowering, the vine grower should select only the shoots that will be useful in producing quality grapes: this selection is carried out by bud removal and desuckering. The shoots grow fast — from 5 to 15 centimeters a day. It is therefore necessary to raise them and tie them regularly to the trellising before it is time to trim them.

JUNE

Flowering starts in May and extends into June; the vine plant enters its reproductive cycle. This is a key period exerts a direct influence on the quantity and quality of grapes, and on the date of harvest. The success of this stage depends on the weather conditions. Cold weather and rain during pollination may induce *coulure*, resulting in uneven formation of berries in a cluster, or *millerandage*, resulting in insufficiently developed berries.

JULY

Once the flowering is over, fruit set follows: the flowers turn into berries. From this moment, vine growers have a fairly clear idea of the harvest date, even if it is three months away, since peak ripeness occurs 120 days after flowering (this is a constant, especially for black merlot) and 45 days after the demi-véraison, or halfway through the fruit set period (see August, below). During this time when the vines are very sensitive to fungal or mite attacks, the winemaker makes sure that the plants get sufficient, but not excessive, pest control protection. For several years, major efforts have been made to limit treatments to a minimum. In addition, operations of lifting (maintaining the canes inside the trellis system) and topping (trimming the upper canes) are carried out regularly as the vine grows.

Finally, July and August is a key period determining the quality of the vintage. In July, at fruit set, leaf pulling is performed on the plots facing east (where the sun rises) to ensure maximum exposure to light, and the vines are trimmed of any excess clusters of grapes (green harvest). (See pages 96-99, "Crop control: mastering the plant".)

AUGUST

As the fruit develops, the berries change color and start to mature. The duration of this stage depends on the weather conditions and this in turn influences the quality of the harvest. Additionally, it is at this moment that the vine stops growing. The canes change color, going from green to brown: this is called *aoûtement*. August is also the month when the second stage of leaf pulling is done, this time on the west-facing side of the rows. Any clusters whose berries do not show a homogeneous development are also green-harvested (removed) so that ripening can be concentrated on the remaining fruit.

SEPTEMBER

Once the canes have turned brown, the vine grower gets ready for the harvest. His chief concern is to choose the right date to harvest perfectly ripe, healthy grapes, devoid of any grey rot. This is not an easy decision, for every year is different. Each vintage is a different case. Ripeness levels are checked and berries are tasted at regular intervals. When the official beginning of the harvest is declared (see page 100), the grape harvest may start. It will last for one to three weeks depending on the size of the vineyard and on the weather conditions.

THE PEOPLE BEHIND BORDEAUX WINES

They are one of the three elements of Bordeaux's magical equation: wine growers, château owners, cellar masters, vineyard managers, wine traders, and vineyard workers all share the same passion — the wines of Bordeaux, which they made famous. "The art of making Bordeaux wines", says Jonathan, a winemaker in the Bordeaux AOC, "is the joy of transmitting knowledge from one generation to the next, no matter whether the vintage is excellent or difficult — the joy of knowing every nook and cranny of our plots." The Bordeaux vineyard is home to many families who have been cherishing their precious terroir and winemaking skills for centuries, eagerly keeping that heritage alive, and preserving the balance of tradition and modernity throughout the generations. Women are increasingly represented in the Bordeaux wine world — as wine growers, winemakers, oenologists, cellar masters, estate owners or administrators, they are now recognized as part of a trade that has long been the privilege of men. Young couples are also contributing to the vitality of the vineyard, as well as people who, while not born into the world of winemaking, gave in to the call of the vineyard and of the attractive Bordeaux region. These men and women decide to live a new life and become winemakers, making their dream a reality and living their passion to its full extent.

Discover some video portraits of winemakers on www.bordeaux.com

SUSTAINABLE DEVELOPMENT IN THE BORDEAUX VINEYARD

In the constantly changing Bordeaux wine region, the methods inherited from former generations of winemakers go hand in hand with the most recent technical innovations: thus, the art of wine benefits from the latest progress in the scientific knowledge on vine, grapes, soil types, and winemaking. For instance, malolactic fermentation — a natural fermentation process occurring after alcoholic fermentation — was not widely known before the 1950s nor fully controlled before the 1970s. The knowledge of grape maturation and of the polyphenols contained in the skins and seeds made tremendous progress towards the end of the 20th century. All that contributed to a steady improvement of the wines and to a greater consistency of quality. Along with this constant learning of skills and knowledge, and partly as a result of that learning, the new generation of Bordeaux winemakers is characterized by an increased concern for the environment and the biological integrity of both the vine plant and wine. For over twenty years, the Interprofessional Council of Bordeaux Wines has been monitoring the impact of the winemaking trade on the environment. In 2010, following research on the carbon footprint of Bordeaux wines and the Plan Climat Bordeaux 2020, it created the initiative of an original environmental approach based on the pooling and sharing of experiences — the Environmental Management System (SME) of Bordeaux wines. This collective tool for environmental improvement is meant to be adapted to every wine grower and trader in order to benefit the entire wine trade. It helps wine professionals adopt a global environmental approach to their estate or their business, particularly in order to share costs (purchase of equipment, regulatory watch, professional training...), preserve the quality and diversity of soils, keep the ecosystem healthy, increase the quality of air and water, and promote the exchange of experience and expertise within the trade — in short, to foster their involvement in sustainable development.

INTEGRATED VITICULTURE, ORGANIC WINEMAKING, AND BIODYNAMY

All three terms refer to different approaches used by winemakers to tend their vineyards and produce their wine with maximum respect for the environment. They differ from one another by their methodology. Each one is defined by a precise set of criteria.

Integrated agriculture, as defined by a decree published in the *Journal Officiel* of April 28, 2002, is a comprehensive approach aiming to enhance the positive impacts of agricultural practices on the environment and to minimize their negative effects. In the vineyard, it manifests itself primarily via integrated pest control, a technique which is widely adopted throughout the Bordeaux region and is founded on the use of selected pesticides which have minimal impact on the environment. They are used in association with a regular, comprehensive and detailed inspection of the vineyard. Besides integrated pest control, this type of viticulture is also based on biological control (using living organisms to reduce the damage caused by pests), which is also practiced by organic viticulture. This method makes use of beneficial insects (ladybugs, dragonflies, wasps) that devour caterpillars, worms, mealybugs and moths, all harmful to the vine. In addition, installing beehives or sowing honey plants near the vineyard help to encourage bee pollination.

Organic viticulture, ruled by the European CE 2092/911 regulation, requires the use of products which are free of any synthetic organic molecules and permits only the use of raw materials of natural origin (mineral or vegetable). The aim is to take special care of the soil and promote the natural ecosystem. Compliance with the specification is monitored by accredited certification organizations (Ecocert, Qualité France...) and entitles the farmer or winemaker to display the words "organic farming" and the AB logo.

The principle of biodynamic viticulture is based on favoring the balance between the vine and its environment. This approach was outlined in 1924 under the influence of Austrian philosopher and agronomist Rudolf Steiner, through a series of lectures to farmers. It advocates the improvement ("revitalization") of soils and plants by plowing with the addition of vegetable, animal and mineral-based mixtures, and by applying these at specific moments of the vine's growth cycle, defined by the lunar and planetary calendars. Biodynamic production is managed by the international Demeter label.

PRUNING, TRAINING AND OTHER VINEYARD WORK

Pruning and training are critical operations; the quality of the next harvest depends on them. The vine grower will devote his entire attention to them, along with other vineyard tasks performed to optimize the final quality of the wine.

A FEW LOCAL PRUNING TERMS

Aste: from the Gascon *asta*, itself from the Latin *hasta*, meaning "shaft" or "stem". A shoot or cane expected to bear fruit, and thus left on the vine during pruning so that new fruiting shoots may grow from it.

Cep: this is the woody stock of the vine plant, which can reach the age of one hundred years. As a rule, older vines produce better, more complex wines than young vines.

Côt, courson or côt de retour: literally a spur, or a cane trimmed to a short stub and left on some stocks to become the fruiting cane in the following year. It generally bears two or three eyes (buds).

PRUNING, FOR STRONGER STOCKS

Long ago, vine growers noticed that stocks whose shoots had been eaten by animals produced larger, better grapes. So they decided to prune the vines to improve their productivity and the quality of their fruit. Indeed, pruning balances the vegetative growth of the vine stock and concentrates the sap that runs through the shoots, making them stronger.

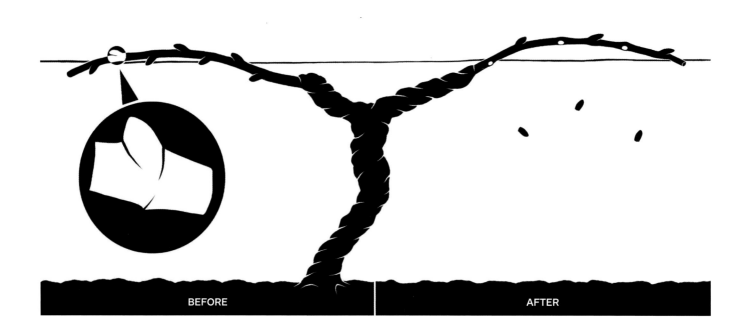

BEFORE

AFTER

BORDELAIS TRAINING OR MÉDOC TRAINING

The Bordelais training or Médoc training has a two-armed, fan-shaped aspect. It may be mistaken for spur training, for each cordon (main branch) bears a cane with six or seven buds depending on the grape variety, however all the buds facing the ground are removed so that only two or three are left on each cane. The upper end of the cane can be partly twisted around the lower wire of the training system, and secured in place. To insure proper cane renewal, keeping spurs with two eyes (or dormant buds) is allowed on up to 25% of the stocks.

GUYOT TRAINING

Guyot training is practiced on all grape varieties and on the entire Bordelais terroir, the only variation being the choice of the single or double Guyot form depending on soil fertility and grape variety. The principle of single Guyot is as follows: each year, one long cane bearing six to ten buds is kept and trained horizontally, or slantwise, or vertically, or arched towards the ground; a two-budded spur is also kept for the growth of a new cane in the following year. After each harvest, the long cane is pruned out. Double Guyot, as the name implies, is composed of two single Guyots on the same vine stock — that is to say, one cane and one spur on either side of the stock. In vineyards of medium-density planting, this type of training allows for a regular distribution of the harvest, insuring optimal maturing of the grapes.

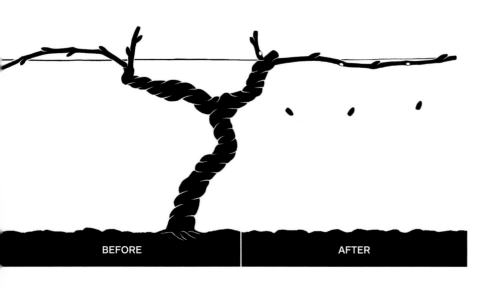

BEFORE

AFTER

CORDON TRAINING

This type of training is sometimes practiced in the Médoc and in some parts of the Blayais, but it is by no means the most common in the region. It consists in a vertical stock prolongated by a permanent horizontal cane on which five to seven fruiting spurs are left.

LYRE TRAINING

Rarely used in the Bordeaux region, this type of training is included here to complete the picture. Lyre training is the only one that allows for proper exploitation of wide-shaped vines. A lyre shape is formed from two axes of trellising. Two branches perpendicular to the vine row bear either spurs or canes that are tied to the trellising. This shape gives the vine an open structure and insures that all the clusters get enough sun.

CROP CONTROL WORK: MASTERING THE PLANT

Crop control work, developed by Bordeaux winegrowers over the last few decades, is a collection of operations directly performed on the vines as they grow. The objective is to obtain the best grape quality by promoting the ripening of berries, improving the vine's health and limiting sap consumption. Here are the main crop control operations:

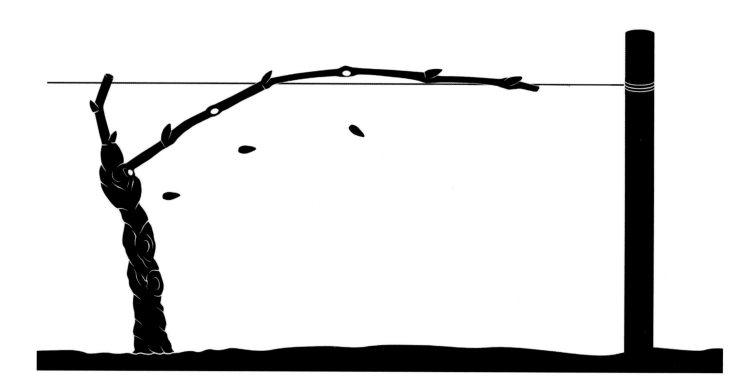

DEBUDDING AND DESUCKERING

Right after bud break, it is important to remove any buds and shoots that are surplus to fruit production so that the plant may devote its energy to those that will bear fruit. This should not be done too early, for no wine grower is safe from climatic incidents such as frost or hail.

De-budding consists of removing some of the buds on the canes left after pruning, or the shoots that have grown from them a few days after bud break. Desuckering is the removal of suckers, which are shoots appearing on old canes, trunk and cordons.

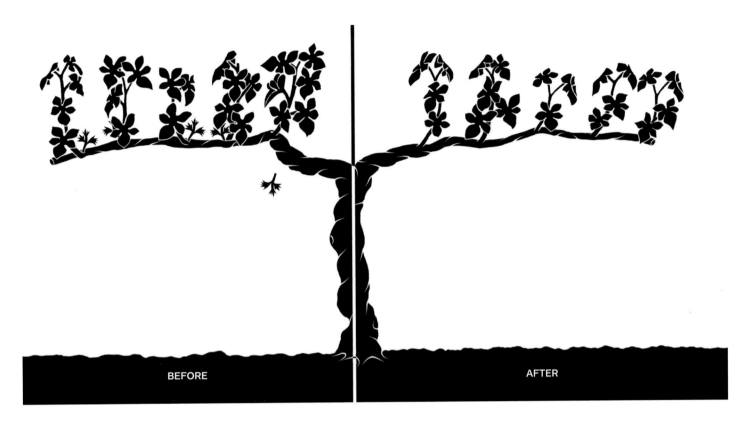

BEFORE

AFTER

DÉDOUBLAGE

A variation on desuckering, it is a French term that may be translated as "removing duplicate shoots". Each bud has a twofold structure, consisting of one main bud and one counter-bud. The counter-bud is, so to speak, the bud's "spare wheel" in case of frost or hail. If such climatic incidents do not happen, this counterbud should be eliminated so that it does not interfere with the growth of the fruiting shoot.

Crop control plays a crucial part in vine growing by helping the grapes reach optimal maturity

LIFTING

During its vegetative period, the vine grows fast. The vine grower has to control its shape by keeping the canes inside the trellis system. This operation consists of "sculpting" the vine into rows, also facilitating the passing of machinery.

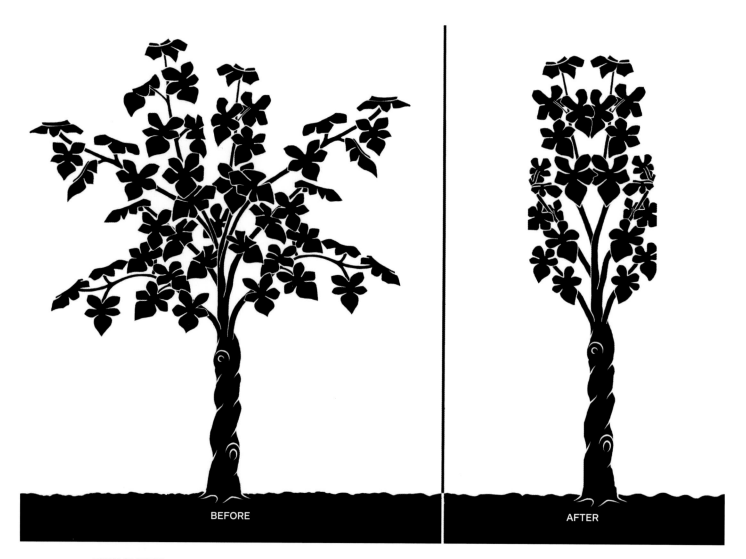

BEFORE

AFTER

TRIMMING

Once the vine is secured in the trellis system, it keeps growing more or less steadily. The vine grower has to trim the shoots to keep the leaf surface constant.

DE-LEAFING

In order to promote both the ripening and healthy development of grapes, some leaves should be eliminated at cluster level. Once that barrier has been removed, the grapes get better sunlight exposure and ripen more easily. This technique has another useful effect: the clusters are better ventilated, thus less sensitive to disease, and less likely to contaminate the whole plot.

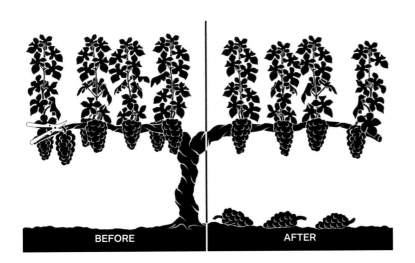

THINNING OR GREEN HARVEST

All the techniques mentioned above are meant to improve grape quality, and therefore wine quality. However, the vitality of the stocks and the obligation to keep the yield at a level defined by the Appellation d'origine contrôlée may lead the vine grower to eliminate some of the harvest later in the season. This method, which would have been unthinkable generations ago, allows the plant to concentrate its strength in a reduced number of grape clusters, which improves their alcoholic and aromatic potential. It also helps in reducing the yield. Thinning, also known as "green harvest", is an important and difficult task — for it is easy to eliminate buds, shoots, or clusters, but achieving an efficient selection for grape quality requires skills and plenty of experience. Some winemakers do not practice green harvest, or do it only on very abundant years.

HARVEST TIME

Harvest is a crucial moment for the winemaker, for it is when the result of a year's hard work comes together. And while grapes are created by nature, it is man who, through his skills, brings out the best in them and turns them into wine. This process begins with the selection of the harvest date — a difficult choice, for grapes must be harvested in a perfect state of health and maturity if one wishes to make an excellent wine.

If grapes are picked too early, insufficient maturity leads to a deficit in sugar and excess acidity, producing thin, harsh wines. Conversely, if the grapes are harvested too late, excessive maturity results in a lack of aromatic content, poor acidity and sugar deficiency. The resulting wines lack aroma, with a possible "stewed" or jammy taste, heaviness and flabbiness in the mouth, and an imbalance between alcoholic content and tannic structure.

In order to select the best harvest dates for each grape variety, it is necessary to follow the maturation of each one starting from the end of August. Plot by plot, once or twice a week, samples of grape clusters or berries are taken to extract the juice and determine, by chemical analysis, the sugar and acid levels, maturity being the right balance of these two parameters. Recently, the monitoring of phenolic maturity (see text to the right) has enabled winemakers to fine-tune the decision. However, these tests are not sufficient; nothing replaces the human palate. Tasting the grapes regularly throughout the vineyard to check the cellular maturity of the berries remains essential.

Each year, the Technical Committee for the Inventory of Vineyard Maturity of the Gironde lists all the tests performed on plots to visualize the status of different varieties as precisely as possible. For harvest to begin, each AOC requires a mandatory level of sugar concentration for each grape variety. Each wine grower is supposed to check on — alone, or with the assistance of his usual consulting laboratory — the ripeness of his grapes and make the right decision concerning the harvest date according to specifications of the appellation. However, the authorized inspection agency may submit his grapes to random spot checks to ensure that the maturity requirements are respected. Once harvesting is allowed, on the basis of chemical tests, weather forecasts, and tasting the grapes, each winemaker sets the first day of his own harvest according to the varieties he grows and the particularities of his own terroirs.

PHENOLIC MATURITY

For a long time, only the pulp of grapes was tested to evaluate ripeness. In the late 1990s, thanks to research done in Bordeaux with the help of the CIVB, winemakers realized that phenolic maturity should also be checked. Phenolic maturity is the optimal levels of polyphenols (tannins and anthocyanins) contained in the skins, pips and stems. Since the collection of these data has been mastered, wines have generally become rounder, deeper and more delicate.

HOW WINE IS BORN

From maceration to fermentation, from blending to aging, man takes over from nature to turn the grapes from fruit to wine, with the aim to achieve the optimal expression of terroir.

The various vinification methods, many of which were invented or improved upon in Bordeaux, are intended to draw out the distinctive features and natural qualities of the grapes. However advanced technology is, it should always be at the service of soil and nature. The grapes are harvested plot by plot, variety by variety, then, once they arrive at the cellar, they follow parallel winemaking circuits based on grape variety and terroir. The winemaker directs every step of the vinification and aging process, relying first and foremost on preliminary tastings and on his expertise.

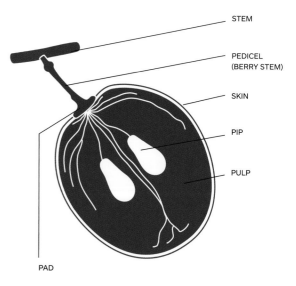

STEM

PEDICEL
(BERRY STEM)

SKIN

PIP

PULP

PAD

MAKING RED WINE

Red Bordeaux wines are made from dark-skinned grapes with clear juice. In order to give them their color and tannins, the pigments contained in the skin have to be transferred to the must through maceration. From this maceration depends the tannic and aromatic framework of a red wine.

1. *Stemming and crushing.* Hand-harvested grapes are sent to a de-stemmer to separate the berries from the stems (the whole stalk system connecting the berries to the cane). After being sorted to remove unripe or damaged fruit, the berries are passed through a crusher where they are lightly crushed, not mashed, to release the juice. However, not all winemakers practice crushing: some prefer to send the uncrushed berries directly into the fermenting vats to respect the integrity of the grape. All the juice, skins and pips — or uncrushed berries — then go into the fermenting vat. In most cases, a little sulfur dioxide (SO_2) is added in order to prevent both the oxidation of the grape's flavors and the development of certain micro-organisms that may affect fermentation. In recent years, at some wineries, alcoholic fermentation has been preceded by a phase of cold prefermentary maceration (sometimes called a cold soak) using dry ice to control the temperature. This operation aids the selective diffusion of certain compounds in the grape such as flavors and pigments.

2. *Alcoholic maceration and fermentation (first fermentation).* The fermentation tank may be made of wood, stainless steel, or plain or coated concrete. It may have a variety of shapes: recently, the egg-shaped concrete vat has become rather popular, while in general, wood and concrete have been enjoying a revival. Nowadays, most vats are internally or externally thermoregulated, which allows, among other things, temperature control during alcoholic fermentation. Cold prefermentary maceration and alcoholic fermentation are carried out together on a monovarietal basis: one vat may only contain the juice of one grape variety and, preferably, of one single plot. At this point, blending has not happened yet. The must (grape juice) and skins (the whole skin mass is also known as pomace or marc) macerates for twenty-one days, sometimes longer, depending on the intended type of wine. These phases of prefermentary and fermentary maceration allow the extraction of pigments and tannins from the skin to the juice. After a few days in the vat, the must begins to ferment under the natural action of grape yeasts. Alcoholic fermentation starts above 16 to 18 °C (60 to 64 °F) and may reach about 28 to 30 °C

THE ROLE OF THE CONSULTANT OENOLOGIST

Bordeaux wine properties regularly hire the services of consultant oenologists, usually for a long-term collaboration. However, the role played by this consultant is little known to the general public. He has sometimes been accused — on the basis of media works bordering on caricature — of "shaping" the wine according to a predefined style and thus of contributing to a globalization of taste. Yet this hasty judgment may easily be modified by experience: several wineries located next door to one another can share the same oenologist and still produce totally different wines. Actually, terroir always rules: the role of the consultant oenologist is to analyze the data in a vineyard in order to reach a global view of it, from which he will advise the resident team in order to help them develop the essential character of their terroir. He always puts himself and his passion for wine at the service of the property that hires him, and strives to let it express its true nature. His advice may include selecting grape varieties to be planted, harvest dates for different plots, managing fermentation and extraction during winemaking, or aging methods... He works in harmony with the vineyard managers and cellar masters, who are in charge of the vineyard and of the winemaking process respectively.

(82 to 86 °F; it may be controlled through thermoregulation as necessary), for an average duration of 18 days. Through that process, the sugars contained in the grapes are turned into alcohol while carbon dioxide and heat are also released.

During this stage, the pomace (the skin and pips) converges towards the top part of the vat into a mass that is called a "cap". Specific techniques are used to facilitate the extraction of the grape components by immersing the cap and preventing the growth of harmful bacteria that are likely to proliferate in the solid parts emerging above the must; pumping-over consists of pumping the juice from the bottom to the top of the vat and pouring it over the cap. *Delestage* or "rack and return" consists of emptying all the juice from the vat by gravity, at the end of which the cap is pressed by its own weight when it settles at the bottom of the vat. Then the juice poured out of the vat is poured back in from the top so that the cap is fully immersed. *Pigeage*, or punching–down, is a very old technique that inspired the two previously mentioned methods: using a *pige* (pestle) held at arm's length through the opening of the vat (or using a mechanical *pige*), the winemaker breaks and immerses the cap.
After the first fermentation, an extra postfermentary maceration may follow, also under temperature control, so that the wine's tannins have a chance to build a complete structure.

3. *Drawing off and pressing.* The fermented must is separated from the pomace (skin + pips) before being transferred into another vat. At this stage, it is known as free-run wine. Then the pomace is gently pressed to extract the remaining juice: this is called press wine. Pneumatic or hydraulic presses are used for this purpose. During blending, the more tannic and deeply-colored press wine may be added in varying proportions to the free-run wine depending on the type of wine one wishes to obtain.

RED WINEMAKING

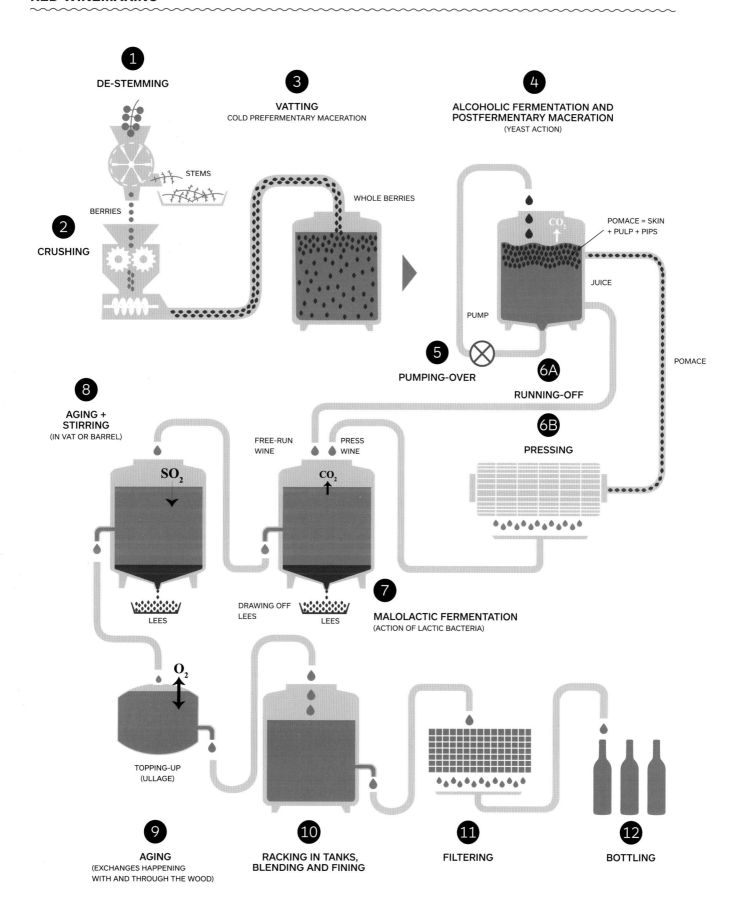

1 DE-STEMMING

STEMS

BERRIES

2 CRUSHING

3 VATTING
COLD PREFERMENTARY MACERATION

WHOLE BERRIES

4 ALCOHOLIC FERMENTATION AND POSTFERMENTARY MACERATION
(YEAST ACTION)

CO_2

POMACE = SKIN + PULP + PIPS

JUICE

PUMP

5 PUMPING-OVER

6A RUNNING-OFF

POMACE

6B PRESSING

8 AGING + STIRRING
(IN VAT OR BARREL)

SO_2

FREE-RUN WINE

PRESS WINE

CO_2

DRAWING OFF LEES

LEES

LEES

7 MALOLACTIC FERMENTATION
(ACTION OF LACTIC BACTERIA)

O_2

TOPPING-UP (ULLAGE)

9 AGING
(EXCHANGES HAPPENING WITH AND THROUGH THE WOOD)

10 RACKING IN TANKS, BLENDING AND FINING

11 FILTERING

12 BOTTLING

4. *Second fermentation.* Known as malolactic fermentation, this second fermentation takes place after alcoholic fermentation. It contributes to the successful evolution of the wine by reducing its acidity, due to bacteria that convert malic acid into lactic acid, also with a release of carbon dioxide. This second fermentation may be carried out either in vats or in barrels. As blending has not taken place yet, free-run wine and press wine can undergo their *malo* separately.

5. *Racking.* Once the two fermentations are complete, the wine is racked: it is separated from its lees (dead yeast cells), which settle in the bottom of the vat or barrel. During the racking, the wine is slightly sulfited, which helps to stabilize it, protecting it against oxidation and possible risks of alteration by some micro–organisms. At this stage, a range of separate wine vats is used.

6. *Aging.* Wine is a living product. During the aging stage, it is clarified and matures after undergoing many internal biochemical transformations. The aging of red wine is done in vats and/ or in oak barrels, for an average duration of twelve to eighteen months in Bordeaux. During this period, depending on changes in atmospheric pressure and temperature, the wine expands or condenses: this causes air pockets — which are potential sources of wine spoilage — to form at the top of the containers. To prevent this, one must ensure that the containers are always full to the brim by frequently pouring in a little extra wine — this is called topping-up or ullage. During winter, the wine is clarified by natural settling, then it is fined with egg white, which attracts any particles remaining in suspension in the wine. Finally, throughout aging, between 2 and 4 rackings are necessary, with or without aeration, to promote the maturation of the wine and eliminate excess lees by adding oxygen in small amounts. When these operations are done, the wine is ready for the final blending.

THE VIRTUES OF GRAVITY-LED FERMENTATION

This slightly obscure term covers an increasingly common and popular method in Bordeaux, though it is hardly new. The aim is to avoid excess handling of the grapes and to submit them to as little manipulation as possible before vatting, whether they are crushed or not. To achieve this, natural gravitation is used — the grapes move under the action of their own weight, with the aim to keep the fruit intact. At the end of the 19th century, there were already some gravitary vathouses in the Bordeaux region. The technical advances of cast-iron architecture at that period allowed the building of light, flexible and strong structures that made this type of installation possible. The principle is simple: reception of harvested grapes, de-stemming, sorting and crushing are done at ground level or upstairs, and the grapes are then carried directly into the vats below through openings in the floor. Beautiful examples of gravity-led vathouses dating from that period may be seen at Château Pontet-Canet and Château Lynch-Bages (Pauillac), as well as at Château Desmirail and Château Malescot-Saint-Exupéry (Margaux).

This method was never forgotten: all modern vathouses use the gravity method, sometimes conceived in a more or less theatrical way by cutting-edge architect-designers, as can be seen at Château La Lagune (Haut-Médoc) where long pivoting metallic arms carry the grapes into large stainless steel vats, or at Château Cos-d'Estournel (Saint-Estèphe) where winemaking is done entirely by gravity, without a single pump, through elevator-vats in a state-of-the-art stainless steel vathouse. This is the paradox of technology, whose refinements are designed for minimal intervention on the raw material in order to reflect the terroir in the best possible way.

Wine is a living product. During its aging stage, it is clarified and starts acquiring a certain degree of maturity.

MAKING DRY WHITE WINE

In Bordeaux, all dry white wines are made from white grapes. Unlike red wine, what is sought here is not to extract any color or tannins: therefore, any sort of maceration is avoided. As for red wines, the winemaker directs every step of the vinification and aging processes, relying primarily on tasting and on his experience.

1. *De-stemming, crushing, pressing.* In most cases, upon their arrival in the cellar, white grapes are de-stemmed and crushed, then immediately pressed to release the must and discard all skins in order to prevent maceration. The juice is then quickly and lightly sulfited to delay the onset of fermentation and reduce oxidation. In some cases, cold skin maceration (prefermentary maceration) is done as a variation of traditional vinification, so that a maximum amount of primary aromas contained in the skins may be extracted while the berries are inside the vat and at a cold temperature before they are pressed.

PLOT BY PLOT

"The ideal vathouse should be exactly superimposed upon the vineyard's plot structure", says Patrick Maroteaux, the owner of Château Branaire-Ducru in Saint-Julien-Beychevelle, referring to one of the great recent innovations in winemaking. Instead of mixing the harvest from all the plots in large vats, winemakers are now trying to ferment homogeneous lots from definite plots in smaller units. Aside from an increase in the aromatic purity of the must, this method allows winemakers to identify and sometimes discard parts of the vintage that have not been harvested at perfect levels of maturity. This type of separated vinification helps to improve selection and blending, and to produce more delicate and complex wines.

WHITE WINEMAKING

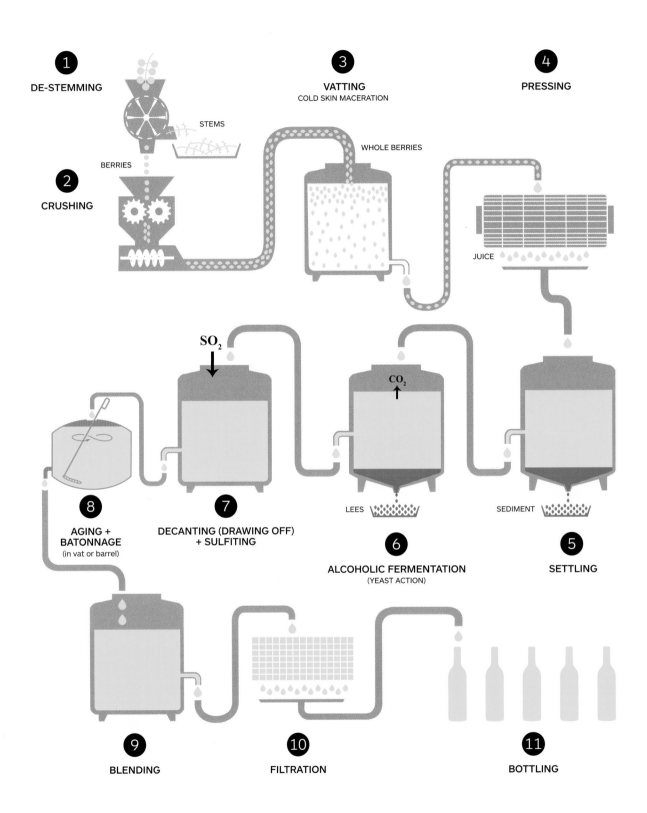

1 DE-STEMMING

STEMS

BERRIES

2 CRUSHING

3 VATTING
COLD SKIN MACERATION

WHOLE BERRIES

4 PRESSING

JUICE

SO₂

8 AGING + BATONNAGE
(in vat or barrel)

7 DECANTING (DRAWING OFF) + SULFITING

CO₂

LEES

6 ALCOHOLIC FERMENTATION
(YEAST ACTION)

SEDIMENT

5 SETTLING

9 BLENDING

10 FILTRATION

11 BOTTLING

LESS SULFUR!

For today's winemakers, using less sulfur is a challenge that must be met. However useful the compound is, it is now well known that lowering the amount of added sulfur helps to emphasize the natural fruitiness of the wine. Many winemakers are now interested in maximizing fruit and freshness, and an increasing number of consumers are also sensitive to sulfur. For the last forty years or so, the global SO2 input in winemaking has decreased by 30 to 60%.

2. *Settling.* The purpose of this operation is to rid the must of suspended particles, or *bourbes* in French. It is usually done by natural decantation at a low temperature. At the end of the settling, racking is carried out to separate the clear juice from the deposit that has settled at the bottom of the vat.

3. *Alcoholic fermentation.* This is carried out on clear must, without any skins or suspended particles, at a lower temperature than for red wine fermentation (from 16 to 18 °C — 60 to 64 °F), for an average duration of twelve to fifteen days. Malolactic fermentation, which is mandatory for red wines, is optional in the case of whites, for it raises the risk of an excess lowering of the wine's acidity. Actually, its advisability depends on the grape variety and above all on the intended style of wine.

4. *Drawing off, sulfiting.* Once fermentation is complete, the wine should be separated from its coarser lees by drawing off and sulfiting. Refrigeration or filtration is helpful in removing the finer lees, which are not always eliminated when the wine is aged on lees.

5. *Aging.* New wines all need to be prepared for blending, bottling and consumption. Aging has the effect of clarifying and stabilizing them, eliminating their youthful failings and giving them a chance to blossom out. Like red wines, white wines may be aged in vats or in oak barrels.

6. *Blending.* As is also the case for red wines, this operation aims at balancing the grape varieties, terroirs and harvest dates by elaborating one or several cuvées. It is followed by filtration — in most cases —, and then by bottling.

The alcoholic fermentation of white wines is done on clear must for an average duration of twelve to fifteen days.

MAKING SWEET WHITE WINES (MOELLEUX OR LIQUOREUX)

Sweet white wines, whether they are moelleux (semi-sweet) or liquoreux (sweet), are made from grapes affected by noble rot, which concentrates juice and flavors. Unlike dry white wines, which contain less than 4 grams of sugar per liter after fermentation, these wines are characterized by an amount of residual (unfermented) sugar of 4 grams per liter or above, and a high alcohol content, in balance with the high amount of residual sugar. For moelleux whites, the amount of residual sugar is between 4 and 45 grams per liter, whereas for *liquoreux* whites, it is required to be a minimum 45 g per liter. Upon their arrival at the winery, the grapes are not de-stemmed but quickly pressed. Pressing is slow and difficult due to the extreme concentration of the juice, which limits the flow. After a phase of settling, the must ferments slowly. However, for the sweet wine to reach a good balance of alcohol and unfermented sugar, the fermentation often has to be interrupted before its natural completion. The wine is then drawn off, cooled and sulfited. Then begins the aging phase, significantly longer for these types of wines than for reds or dry whites (usually two years for *liquoreux*).

ROSÉ WINEMAKING - Press method

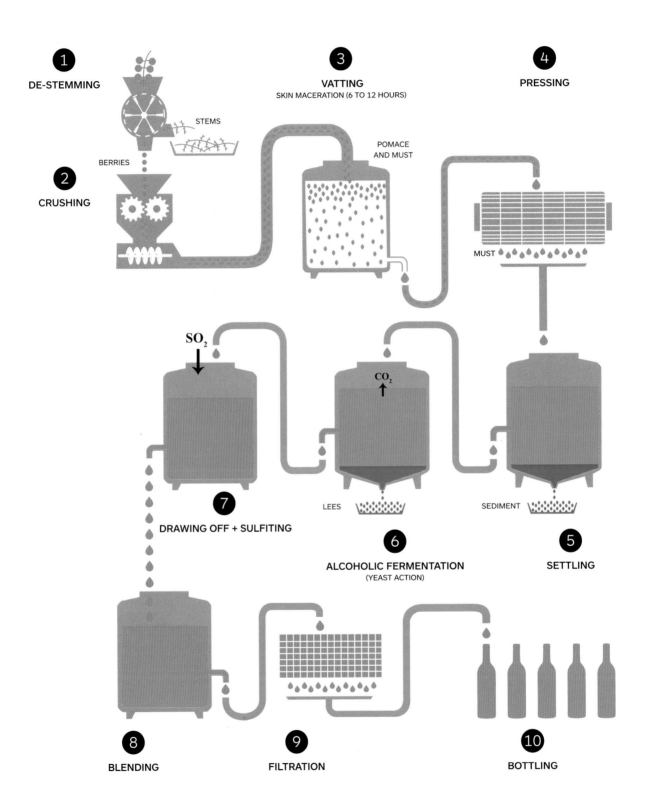

1 DE-STEMMING

2 CRUSHING

BERRIES

STEMS

3 VATTING
SKIN MACERATION (6 TO 12 HOURS)

POMACE AND MUST

4 PRESSING

MUST

SO_2

7 DRAWING OFF + SULFITING

CO_2

LEES

6 ALCOHOLIC FERMENTATION
(YEAST ACTION)

SEDIMENT

5 SETTLING

8 BLENDING

9 FILTRATION

10 BOTTLING

MAKING ROSÉ OR CLAIRET WINES

Contrary to what some people believe, a rosé is not a blend of red wine and white wine: it is based on the pressing of white-juiced, dark-skinned grapes, and the winemaking is done in a specific manner. In Bordeaux, there are two types of rosés.

• Bordeaux rosé. The juice extraction may be done by pressing the grapes or, more traditionally, by "bleeding", or tapping the vat (*rosé de saignée* or tapping rosé). In the latter case, grapes are de-stemmed and crushed, and then transported into vats as for red wine. After a short, 12-hour maceration, a quantity of juice amounting to 15 to 25% of the vat content is tapped off. This pale pink-colored juice, which contains no tannins, is fermented at a temperature of 16 to 18 °C (60 to 64 °F). Malolactic fermentation is generally avoided in order to preserve the wine's fresh taste.
• Bordeaux clairet. This is an old traditional Bordeaux specialty, halfway between a rosé and a red wine, achieved by bleeding (tapping) after a longer maceration than for rosés (from 24 to 36 hours). This vividly colored, slightly tannic juice is fermented at a temperature of 18 to 20 °C (82 to 86 °F). Malolactic fermentation is generally opted for, giving the wine smoothness and roundness.

MAKING CRÉMANT WINE

Crémants are sparkling wines that can be white or rosé, made according to specifications applied to all French wines of that category. The grapes are harvested by hand when optimally mature, and carried in unsealed containers to let some juices flow out. The grapes are then pressed whole, without any de-stemming or crushing.
The base wine used for the fabrication of Crémant de Bordeaux is a still wine that has undergone alcoholic fermentation in vats, but no malolactic fermentation. After that fermentation, several base wines may be blended together to make a cuvée. The resulting wine should have a minimal alcoholic strength of 10%. After January 1st of the year following the harvest, the base wine is bottled for a second fermentation. A *liqueur de tirage* containing sugar and yeast is added. This secondary alcoholic fermentation, carried out in bottle at low temperature (10 to 12 °C, 50 to 54 °F), aims to help achieve a minimum alcoholic strength of 11%

and to create carbon dioxide pressure inside the bottle.

After being laid down on racks (i.e. kept on their lees) for a minimum period of nine months, the bottles are slightly inclined and gently riddled to bring the yeast deposit down to the neck of the bottle, where it will be eliminated by disgorging.

Once disgorging is complete, the wine is topped up with a *liqueur d'expédition*, whose sugar contents depends on the desired type of sparkling wine — extra-brut, brut, dry, semidry or sweet.

Bordeaux clairet is an ancient tradition, halfway between a rosé and a red wine.

ROSÉ WINEMAKING - Tapping or saignée method

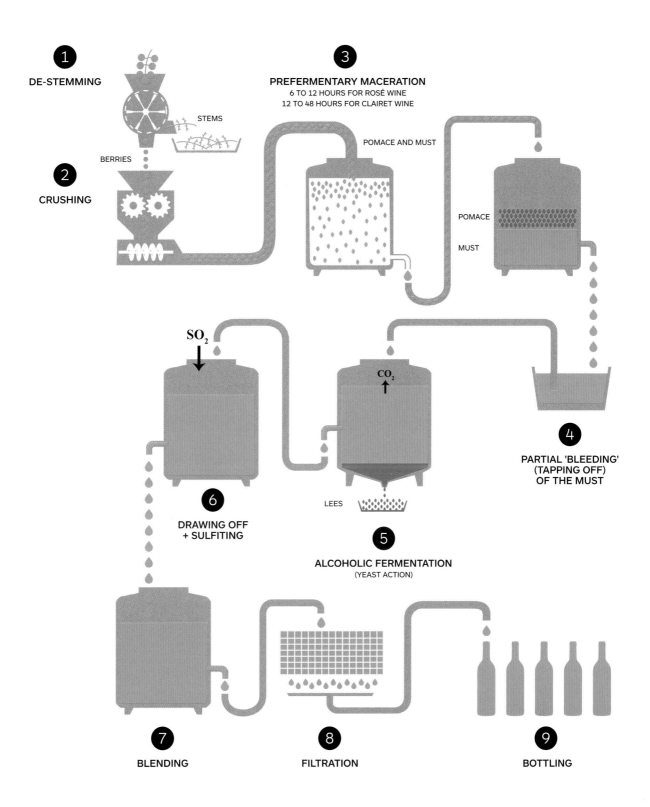

1 DE-STEMMING

STEMS

BERRIES

2 CRUSHING

3 PREFERMENTARY MACERATION
6 TO 12 HOURS FOR ROSÉ WINE
12 TO 48 HOURS FOR CLAIRET WINE

POMACE AND MUST

POMACE

MUST

4 PARTIAL 'BLEEDING'
(TAPPING OFF)
OF THE MUST

SO_2

CO_2

6 DRAWING OFF
+ SULFITING

LEES

5 ALCOHOLIC FERMENTATION
(YEAST ACTION)

7 BLENDING

8 FILTRATION

9 BOTTLING

IN THE CELLAR:
TRADITIONAL METHODS AND
STATE-OF-THE-ART
TECHNIQUES

The tremendous evolution of winemaking skills that has taken place in Bordeaux in recent years applies to the cellars as well as to the vineyards. Often initiated by top châteaux that are always on the lookout for innovative ways of improving quality, these new methods are intended to respect the quality of the grapes and to highlight the terroir on which they were grown.

SORTING THE GRAPES

The game begins even before the grapes enter the cellar. Many properties now have sorting tables, installed in the vineyard or at the entrance to the harvest reception area. They generally consist of treadmills, or vibrating tables on which the grapes are spread apart so that any leaves, twigs and, particularly, damaged or immature berries may be discarded, allowing the winemaker to obtain fruit of the best possible quality. This operation, which requires a large and qualified workforce, leads to significant additional costs, but one does not put a price on quality. Increasingly, in the spirit of a non-interventionist approach to winemaking, this sorting is done on berries after de-stemming and immediately before vatting. New technologies (such as optical sorting, densimetric sorting, and others) have also become quite common.

STATE-OF-THE-ART MACERATIONS

It was in Bordeaux that the value of cold skin maceration was highlighted for the first time. This method improves the transmission of aroma precursors — substances that can be found in grape skins and are known to magnify the wine's aromas after alcoholic fermentation — to the must, and produces wines with far more exuberant fragrances. Cold prefermentary maceration is the equivalent for red wines (see page 103).

THE BLENDING TECHNIQUE

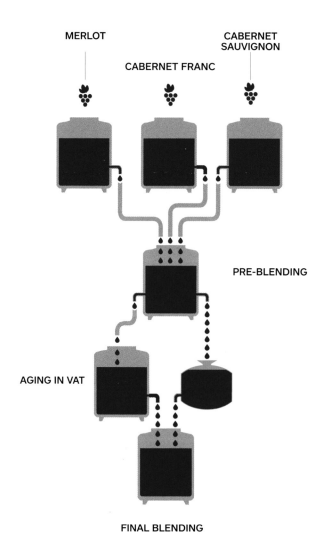

MERLOT

CABERNET FRANC

CABERNET SAUVIGNON

PRE-BLENDING

AGING IN VAT

FINAL BLENDING

STAINLESS STEEL, WOOD OR CONCRETE?

There are many different schools of thought regarding the choice of containers for winemaking, and the dominant position varies with time. The 1970s saw the invasion of stainless steel vats, an innovation that greatly improved hygiene in the cellars. In the 1990s, wooden vats made a reappearance, often in a truncated conic shape. Having the ability to facilitate the exchange of tannins and aromas between the wine and the oak wood, they were primarily used for red wines. In this respect, it should be noted that many white wines are fermented in barrels, and that many wooden vathouses dating from the pre-stainless steel era had never stopped being used, and have stood the test of time. Finally, there is a renewed interest in concrete vats, some of which, again, had continued to be used in the cellars of many prestigious châteaux. Concrete is interesting because it is an inert material that does not affect the taste of wine and allows for better temperature control. However, the traditional form of the cubic concrete tank is now replaced by tapered cylinder or even ovoid shapes, thought to reproduce the physical conditions of ancient amphorae: inside, the must remains in a state of slow rotation that keeps the lees suspended, giving the wine extra body and a velvety texture.

SECRETS OF AGING

For white wines, particularly those aged in barrels for several years, winemakers have recently begun employing the technique of *bâtonnage* associated with aging on lees. It consists of maintaining the wine in contact with its finest lees by frequent stirring. This suspension of the lees has the advantage of promoting a round, fleshy mouthfeel in the wines and preserving aromas. Nowadays, this technique is also sometimes applied to red wines. Great efforts have also been made to better understand the interactions between the juice and the wood during aging — between the famous Bordelais barrel and the wine it contains. Experiments led by some châteaux and the National Institute for Agricultural Research (INRA) have highlighted the positive effect of an early drawing off of the wine from vat after alcoholic fermentation, followed by malolactic fermentation in barrels. The aromatic exchange that takes place during aging is conditioned, among other factors, by the "toast", that is to say the slight bur-

THE CHARACTERISTICS OF GRAPE VARIETIES

Here is a basic description of the qualities of the main — and secondary — grape varieties in a Bordeaux blend. The organoleptic (i.e. sensory) characteristics of each variety will be developed in the next chapter, page 139 (boxed text).

REDS
Cabernet sauvignon: a late, tannic variety; when young, the wines are very aromatic with notes of black fruits and good aging potential.
Merlot: early variety, high alcohol level, elegant tannins, aromatic power (red fruits).
Petit verdot: aromatic power, generosity, pigments, tannins. Some call it a "blend booster". Like other secondary varieties used in Bordeaux such as malbec and carménère, it is known as a "tinctorial" grape for its ability to intensify color.

WHITES
Sémillon: golden color, smooth, delicately aromatic (acacia or lime blossom, ripe pear, green almond, hazelnut). The favorite variety for liquoreux wines.
Sauvignon: pale-colored, high alcohol content, good acidity, richly aromatic (gorse/broom flower, blackcurrant bud, narcissus, jasmine, citrus (lemon or grapefruit), smoky notes. It gives liquoreux wines their mandatory acidic framework. It is the typical variety for dry white wines.
Muscadelle: powerful and rich, moscatel, musky aromas, roundness, low acidity.
Ugni blanc: brings freshness and acidity.

ning applied to the inside of the oak staves that make up the barrel. By painstakingly selecting their aging barrels according to their toast, winemakers influence the aromatic profile of their wines, playing on vanilla or hazelnut notes, or even distinctly toasty notes for dry whites.

A METICULOUS BLEND

We are now reaching a crucial stage of winemaking — the moment when the typicity of a wine and its consistency in quality, elegance and balance are decided. This is the Bordeaux moment *par excellence*, because it was in Bordeaux that the art of blending was first defined and later perfected, through the extended choice of grape varieties of the Gironde.

The choice of variety is determined by the type of wine one wishes to obtain (a dominance of sauvignon for dry white wine, of sémillon for sweet white wine, of merlot for red wines produced on the clay-limestones of the right bank and of cabernet sauvignon for the warm, gravelly soils of the left bank).

During fermentation, each vat contains the specific expression of a terroir through one single grape variety. During aging, the barrels are arranged in such a way that the origin of each must and the plot it was grown on may be easily memorized. Wines from different varieties, obtained from different plots, will later be combined in precise proportions — with the addition of a certain amount of tannic, powerful press wine in the case of red wines — to support the aromatic framework. The wines are tasted separately, then blended in amounts that are redefined each year depending on tasting, to maximize the interactions and complementarity of grape varieties and their original terroirs.

The wine blended in this manner should reflect on a constant basis the individual character of the estate or château, with variations depending on the vintage. It is the expression not only of its terroir but also of its appellation, which implies that some grape varieties dominate the blend — cabernet sauvignon for red wines on the left bank and merlot on the right bank; sémillon and sauvignon for white wines —, while others come in as auxiliary varieties. Auxiliary varieties may also be used for "spicing" (this is the case of muscadelle in white wines) or as a coloring agent (this is the case of petit verdot and malbec for red wines), helping to shape the tannic and aromatic structure, as well as the wine's keeping qualities.

BOTTLING

This stage marks the end of the winemaking process and contributes just like the ones that preceded it to the final quality of the product. Bottling is usually done at room temperature (16-18 °C, 62 to 64 °F) in order to protect the organoleptic qualities of the wine. The containers and corks must be selected according to their ability to preserve the wine in the best possible manner. Whether that operation is carried out in a bottling room at the château or by bottling trucks moving from château to château, the bottles are later transported to the distribution networks or kept in cellars for aging, where the wine will continue its lengthy maturation process.

THE TASTE OF TIME
THE NOTION OF VINTAGE

The reputation of a vintage does not reflect the quality of the wines so much as their ability to age well in bottle. There are good wines in every vintage — the point is to be able to appreciate them at the right time.

Aside from the factors already mentioned, the quality of a wine also depends on nature and on the weather. This explains why no two vintages are alike. In order to obtain a great vintage in red, the crucial determining factors are the following: a rapid, regular flowering; a certain amount of hydric stress in the early stages of the growth cycle in order to limit the volume of berries in August, at fruit set; moderate summer heat with a little rain to ensure complete maturity; and a sunny late season, with cool nights. During the period that separates the maturity of grapes from their optimal overmaturity with a progressive invasion of noble rot, liquoreux wines need sharp temperature contrasts (cool, humid nights; warm, sunny days). Also, for all wines, maturation should be harmonious, without *coulure* (lack of berries in a cluster) or *millerandage* (clusters showing irregular-sized berries).

Overall, in recent years, consistency in vintage quality has increased thanks to the many advances in viticulture and oenology, both in terms of knowledge and of technical mastery. However, each combination of grape variety and terroir reacts individually to weather conditions, and each winemaker relies on his own expertise.

Here are some guidelines that illustrate the general characteristics of recent vintages.

2013: WEAK YIELD

Dry whites: aromatic, fresh, complex wines. Good quality level.

Reds: round and fruity, with a delicate structure. Ready to drink now.

Liquoreux: great vintage with an even spread of botrytis. Pure, concentrated wines with great aromatic complexity.

2012: A WINEMAKERS' VINTAGE

Dry whites: generally excellent. Long-keeping, powerful, aromatic wines.

Reds: good quality on the whole. Balanced, harmonious, long-keeping wines.

Liquoreux: rather good. Round, balanced, nicely "roasted".

2011: A NICE VINTAGE, DRY AND EARLY

Dry whites: super, fruity, powerful wines. To drink within the next few years.

Reds: an even quality with elegance rather than power. Rich, harmonious wines that should be able to age a few years.

Liquoreux: another great year. Generous, rich, complex wines.

2010: A VERY SUCCESSFUL VINTAGE

Dry whites: beautiful, fruity wines with a lot of finesse. To drink within the next few years.

Reds: quite good overall. Strong framework, excellent aging qualities.

Liquoreux: splendid vintage. Round, balanced wines, with lots of roasted notes.

2009: A SUPERB VINTAGE

Dry whites: superb, powerful, aromatic wines. To drink now or to keep.

Reds: very beautiful, full-bodied, structured wines. Will keep a long time.

Liquoreux: exceptional vintage. Very rich, delicate and aromatic wines. Delicious now, but should improve with aging.

2008: A GOOD LATE VINTAGE

Dry whites: a superb vintage. Beautiful, elegant, generous wines.

Reds: quite good overall. Fruity, balanced and rich wines that can age.

Liquoreux: very successful. Extremely rich, concentrated, aromatic wines that will keep for many years.

2007: A GOOD VINTAGE, SAVED BY THE INDIAN SUMMER

Dry whites: an exceptional year. Aromatic, powerful wines.

Reds: a rather even year, with balanced, harmonious wines, to drink now or to keep for a few years.

Liquoreux: a superb years for liquoreux. Rich, complex, concentrated wines, to drink now or to keep.

2006: GOOD OVERALL QUALITY

Dry whites: beautiful, balanced, delicate, elegant wines.

Reds: a lovely vintage. Balanced, rich, harmonious wines, to drink now or to keep. **Liquoreux:** round and balanced, nicely roasted wines. Let them age.

2005: AN EXCEPTIONAL VINTAGE

Dry whites: extremely powerful and concentrated, high in taste, very sappy, with tropical fruit and citrus aromas.

Reds: densely colored, amazing fruit, a lot fresher than 2003, with a remarkable tannic framework.

Liquoreux: very pure and opulent, they have the rich, roasted qualities of the greatest vintages.

2004: UNEVEN QUALITY

Dry whites: very flowery, fruity and delicate; elegant, lengthy wines.

Reds: complex wines in which fruitiness and power merge harmoniously. Good keeping qualities.

Liquoreux: highly aromatic wines, excellent quality on the best terroirs.

2003: EXCELLENT QUALITY, A "WARM" YEAR

Dry whites: aromatic, generally quite successful, with tropical aromatic notes.

Reds: successful on the best terroirs. This vintage is marked by warm, jammy fruit notes and low acidity.

Liquoreux: highly aromatic wines of excellent quality and, on the best terroirs, a rarely attained opulence.

2002: UNEVEN QUALITY

Dry whites: good aromatic intensity, a certain freshness in the structure.

Reds: globally successful, especially cabernets sauvignons, which are rich, harmonious and powerful. Now at their peak.

Liquoreux: uneven wines, medium quality level, but the early lots are superb.

2001: AN UNEVEN VINTAGE

Dry whites: very good wines with a seductive aromatic freshness.

Reds: very uneven quality, although some excellent successes. Fruity, densely colored, tannic wines with a tight, harmonious structure.

Liquoreux: arguably the vintage of the century? Not everyone agrees, but nature has rarely been so generous to winemakers.

2000: EXCEPTIONAL VINTAGE

Dry whites: overall good quality. The wines fully express their aromatic subtlety.
Reds: high in color and tannins, round and fleshy, very flattering, with an intense aromatic freshness. In other terms — a great vintage.
Liquoreux: low yields, uneven quality.

1999: UNEVEN QUALITY

Dry whites: radiantly aromatic, with a precise, nuanced expression of terroir.
Reds: quite concentrated with a beautiful aromatic balance. To drink now.
Liquoreux: concentrated wines with great aromatic complexity.

1998: VERY GOOD QUALITY

Dry whites: aromatic, fresh, more or less full-bodied depending on terroirs.
Reds: beautiful color, nice fruit and good freshness; dense, high-quality tannins. Will age well.
Liquoreux: a lovely aromatic complexity, lots of elegance in the mouth. Can be either concentrated with roasted notes or tender and delicately fruity.

1997: GOOD QUALITY

Dry whites: uneven quality.
Reds: good color, nice fruit, a fleshy, harmonious texture in the mouth although some uneven quality. To drink now.
Liquoreux: good aromatic complexity, smoothness, freshness and elegance in the mouth.

1996: GREAT QUALITY

Dry whites: remarkable by their aromatic richness and vivacity.

Reds: lovely color, lots of fruit, dense wines with a powerful tannic structure.

Liquoreux: confit aromas, very fresh in the mouth, lots of concentration and finesse.

1995: GREAT QUALITY

Dry whites: aromatic, more or less full-bodied depending on terroir.

Reds: lovely color, lots of fruit, a beautiful tannic richness, round tannins.

Liquoreux: lots of concentration, great quality.

1994: GOOD QUALITY

Dry whites: richly aromatic, very balanced in the mouth.

Reds: good; the expression varies with terroir. To drink now.

Liquoreux: uneven, some wines are excellent, but the yield is low.

1993: GOOD QUALITY

Dry whites: very aromatic and balanced.

Reds: lovely color, lots of fruit, balanced and structured, some intensity.

Liquoreux: uneven, medium quality.

1992: MEDIUM, UNEVEN QUALITY

Dry whites: intense, lots of aromatic freshness.

Reds: uneven, smooth, peaking now. To drink now.

Liquoreux: uneven, good quality in the first *tries*.

1991: MEDIUM QUALITY, VERY LOW YIELD

Dry whites: weak yields, uneven quality.

Reds: uneven, with average structure. Drink now.

Liquoreux: uneven, good quality in the first *trie*.

1990: GREAT QUALITY, AN EXCEPTIONALLY RICH VINTAGE

Dry whites: aromatic, rich, smooth and lengthy.

Reds: deep-colored, with excellent, dense, round tannins; a lovely balance.

Liquoreux: aromatic complexity, with the specific roasted aroma of great vintages. Very rich mouthfeel, both smooth and fresh. These wines undoubtedly have a magical touch about them.

THE GREAT WINES OF BORDEAUX - VINTAGE CHART

DRY WHITES

2012 ▲	2011 ▲	2010 ▲	2009 ▲	2008 ■	2007 ▲	2006 ■
2005 ▲	2004 ■	2003 ▲	2002 ●	2001 ■	2000 ■	1999 ■
1998 ■	1997 ●	1996 ■	1995 ■	1994 ■	1993 ●	1992 ■
1991 ●	1990 ●	1989 ■	1988 ■	1987 ■	1986 ■	1985 ●
1984 ●	1983 ■	1982 ●	1981 ■			

LIQUOREUX (SWEET) WHITES

2012 ■	2011 ▲	2010 ■	2009 ▲	2008 ■	2007 ▲	2006 ■
2005 ▲	2004 ●	2003 ▲	2002 ■	2001 ▲	2000 ■	1999 ●
1998 ■	1997 ▲	1996 ■	1995 ■	1990 ▲	1989 ▲	1988 ▲
1986 ■	1985 ■	1983 ▲	1982 ■	1981 ●	1979 ●	1978 ▲
1976 ▲	1975 ▲	1970 ●	1967 ▲	1962 ■	1961 ▲	1959 ▲
1955 ▲	1949 ▲	1947 ▲	1945 ▲	1937 ▲	1929 ▲	1921 ▲

REDS

2012 ■	2011 ■	2010 ▲	2009 ▲	2008 ■	2007 ■	2006 ■
2005 ▲	2004 ■	2003 ▲	2002 ■	2001 ■	2000 ▲	1999 ■
1998 ▲	1997 ■	1996 ▲	1995 ▲	1994 ■	1993 ●	1990 ▲
1989 ▲	1988 ▲	1986 ▲	1985 ■	1983 ■	1982 ▲	1981 ■
1978 ■	1975 ■	1970 ■	1966 ■	1964 ■	1961 ▲	1959 ▲
1955 ▲	1953 ■	1949 ■	1947 ■	1945 ▲	1929 ●	1928 ■

Source: Bordeaux Wine Academy, 2013 edition.

SYMBOLS

 Overall good quality.

 Overall even quality, many excellent bottles.

Uneven quality,
a few lovely bottles.

 They have the fruitiness of young wines and a long future ahead of them.

 They are reaching a stage of maturity and will continue to develop.

 They are coming round nicely and will continue to improve in a good cellar.

 They have reached their peak.

● Fruity, delicate, lively
■ Well-balanced, refined, elegant
▲ Powerful, aromatic, finesse.

● Fine, fruity, elegant
■ Round, well-balanced, with plenty of "rôti"
▲ Full-bodied, robust, complex.

● Delicate, light, and elegant
■ Well-balanced, rich and harmonious
▲ Full-bodied, with a solid structure.

4

FROM THE
CELLAR
TO THE
TABLE

PRINCIPLES OF WINE TASTING

While it is true that tasting requires the use of a specific vocabulary, there is nothing esoteric about it. It is an art that can be mastered with a bit of experience and attention. All the technical data provided serves only one purpose — the pleasure of sharing our experiences around a glass of wine.

Tasting is not the same as drinking. Wine is more than just a beverage: it is a cultural product. Far from being an obscure practice, tasting wine includes different techniques that are accessible to everyone, and teach us to detect, identify and assess the organoleptic qualities of wine (i.e. those that are perceived by our senses). Therefore, it requires the use of our sensory organs, which explains why there is always a subjective aspect to it. Two people can enjoy the same wine in a different manner, depending on to how sensitive they are to certain elements and on their olfactory reference data (for indeed we all have our own olfactory memory). Our ability to identify a perception, acknowledge it and put a name on it directly influences how we experience it. For professionals, tasting requires the acquisition of a specific vocabulary and the mastering of a set of values that is common to all tasters, and learned over time and with practice. While these technical data may seem austere, they have the simple aim of facilitating a conversation about a glass of wine with others.

SUBTLE PARAMETERS

Some frequently overlooked details can modify the experience of wine tasting. Factors such as weather and atmospheric pressure are difficult to assess: a wine does not give the exact same sensations when tasted in cold, brisk weather as when tasted in clear, mild weather. Sometimes it is the environment or the mood of the taster that varies, not the wine, but that can also affect the conclusion. Wearing a heady perfume, standing close to a bouquet of fragrant flowers, or being exposed to other strong odors can also disrupt the olfactory experience. Visual conditions are also crucial: it goes without saying that light is very important in helping to fully perceive the color of a wine. Therefore, be wary of neon lights (which impart a green hue to any color), tinted light bulbs or even colored walls that may alter the light.

HORIZONTAL, VERTICAL...

These terms refer to two different types of tasting: a horizontal tasting brings together several different wines of the same vintage in one geographic production area. The aim is to offer an overview of a precise vintage and terroir, and to recognize the overall style of a vintage in that appellation. A vertical tasting includes several vintages of the same cru or growth; it is a sort of travel through time in search of the specific character of grape varieties, of terroir, and of the winemaker's own style. As a rule, it is advised to start the tasting with the youngest vintage and finish with the oldest one. A vertical tasting of a large number of vintages explores the evolution of a wine throughout its history.

A RELAXED, RECEPTIVE MIND

Since a tasting involves our sensory organs, it is important to approach it in a relaxed manner and when all our senses are fully responsive. Therefore it is better to schedule tastings outside meals in order to concentrate on the wine alone, preferably late morning or late afternoon, when hunger sharpens our senses; and, naturally, to avoid tasting when we are tired or sick, or immediately after having consumed a strong product with a persistent taste, like tobacco, coffee, mint or anise. The best conditions for tasting are to be found in a well-lit location, neither too hot nor too cold, free of any unpleasant smell and as sound-proof as possible. Tasting over a white surface — a table, a tablecloth, a sheet of paper — is recommended in order to appreciate the color of the wine. An adequate number of spittoons should also be provided.

WHICH GLASSES?

The choice of vessels in which to serve the wine is also of great importance. Choose transparent, stemmed glasses, free from any odors. It is better if they bulge at the base and narrow at the rim in order to concentrate the taste of wine in the glass. The tulip-shaped glass is perfectly adapted to Bordeaux wines. Finally, remember that a glass should be filled to one third of its height, never to the top, so that the aromas may concentrate in the top part of the glass. For tasting, one half-inch of wine in the glass is quite enough.

HOW TO STRUCTURE A TASTING

A tasting should be well-organized and structured. The most important point to know is that a wine tasting includes three successive stages:
— The visual stage,
— The olfactory stage,
— The gustatory stage.
If the two former stages involve only one of the senses, the latter involves three: taste, smell and touch. That is what makes it so complex.

DRY WHITE WINES

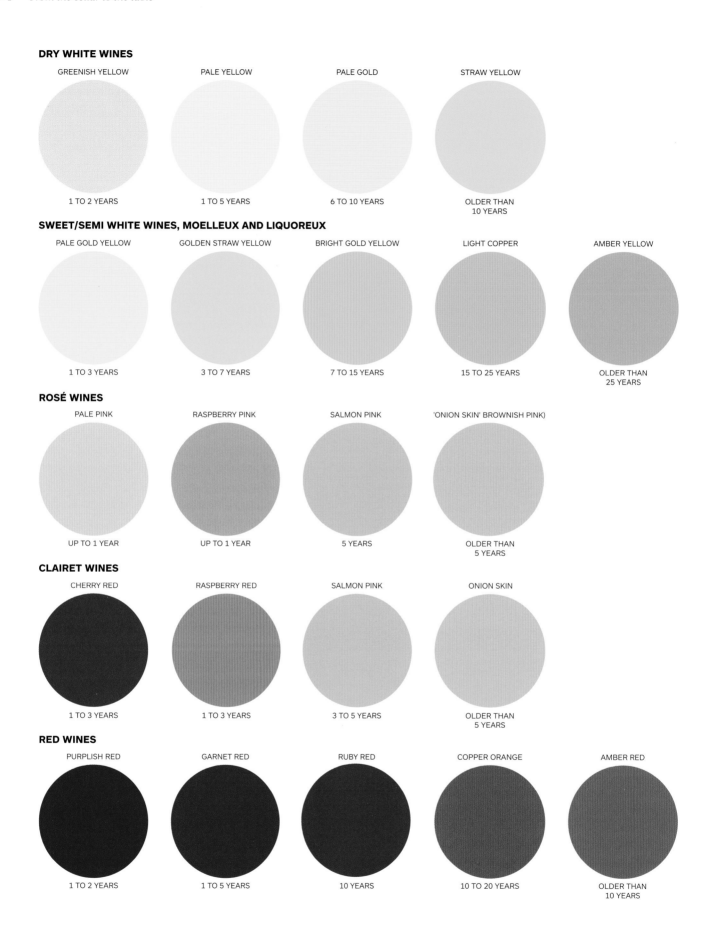

GREENISH YELLOW	PALE YELLOW	PALE GOLD	STRAW YELLOW
1 TO 2 YEARS	1 TO 5 YEARS	6 TO 10 YEARS	OLDER THAN 10 YEARS

SWEET/SEMI WHITE WINES, MOELLEUX AND LIQUOREUX

PALE GOLD YELLOW	GOLDEN STRAW YELLOW	BRIGHT GOLD YELLOW	LIGHT COPPER	AMBER YELLOW
1 TO 3 YEARS	3 TO 7 YEARS	7 TO 15 YEARS	15 TO 25 YEARS	OLDER THAN 25 YEARS

ROSÉ WINES

PALE PINK	RASPBERRY PINK	SALMON PINK	'ONION SKIN' BROWNISH PINK)
UP TO 1 YEAR	UP TO 1 YEAR	5 YEARS	OLDER THAN 5 YEARS

CLAIRET WINES

CHERRY RED	RASPBERRY RED	SALMON PINK	ONION SKIN
1 TO 3 YEARS	1 TO 3 YEARS	3 TO 5 YEARS	OLDER THAN 5 YEARS

RED WINES

PURPLISH RED	GARNET RED	RUBY RED	COPPER ORANGE	AMBER RED
1 TO 2 YEARS	1 TO 5 YEARS	10 YEARS	10 TO 20 YEARS	OLDER THAN 10 YEARS

FIRST STAGE: THE EYE

The visual examination is the first step of tasting. With a little experience, a taster at this stage is able to pick up some valuable clues which will help with the analysis of the next stages. The hue, intensity, clarity and brilliance of wine have to be noted.

• The color of a wine — or, as it is called in French, the *robe* — actually means both the color and the reflections in the wine. The *robe* changes in color and intensity as the wine ages, due to a slight contact with oxygen, via the cork. Therefore, color is a good indicator of the age of a wine. A young red wine tends to have a purple, sometimes blue sheen. As it ages, it develops hints of yellow, which is why a characteristic color in aged red wines is a brownish, orange-red hue, known as "tile red" (*tuilé*).

• The intensity and density of the *robe* reflect the concentration of the wine, which in turn depends on the way it was vinified. For instance, during the fermentation of a red wine, color extraction and material extraction — the extraction of tannins — happen simultaneously during the maceration stage. Therefore, a dense-colored, full-bodied red Bordeaux wine usually has a firm tannic framework. Conversely, a pale-colored, light-bodied wine will have a supple structure.

THE HUES OF WINE

ROSÉS AND CLAIRETS
Salmon pink. Age: from 1 to 3 years. Young wine.
Clairet color (cherry to raspberry). Age: from 1 to 3 years. Young wine.

RED
Purplish red. Age: from 1 to 2 years.
Very young wine.
Ruby red. Age: from 3 to 5 years. Young wine.
Garnet red. Age: from 7 to 10 years. Mature wine.
Copper red. Age: older than 10 years. Aged wine.

DRY WHITES
Pale yellow. Age: from 1 to 2 years. Very young wine.
Straw yellow. Age: from 3 to 5 years. Young wine.

SWEET WHITES
Golden yellow. Age: from 3 to 10 years. Young wine.
Deep gold color. Age: from 10 to 15 years.
Mature wine.
Amber color. Age: older than 15 years. Aged wine.

• Clarity is simply the absence of cloudiness in a wine, its transparency. As a rule, all AOC wine is limpid. However, it may sometimes happen, during aging in bottle, that sudden exposure to cold temperatures or other various incidents can alter the clarity of wine, resulting in the presence of solid particles suspended in the liquid (flyers) or in the bottom of the bottle (color and/ or tartar deposits). In the case of the latter, the wine should be decanted. However, an increasing number of wines — some reds and, more frequently, whites — are not filtered before bottling. This is particularly the case of organic or biodynamic wines; their resultant cloudy appearance is therefore normal and the result of the winemaker's decision. It helps to be aware of the type of wine you are dealing with before reaching for the decanter.

• The brightness or radiance of the color reveals a certain amount of sharpness in the wine, due to its acidity level. Hence, a very bright appearance (especially in white wine) is often the sign of pronounced acidity and of a youthful character, whereas an unshiny color is a sign of full maturity, and a dull, lackluster *robe* indicates that the wine is past its prime. Then again, it should be noted that purposely unfiltered wines have a slightly cloudy appearance. In this case, decanting will not alter the cloudiness.

LEVELS OF INTENSITY IN WINE COLOR

- very dark
  dark
  deep
  dense
  medium
  light
+ pale

LEVELS OF CLARITY IN WINE

- transparent
  clear
  hazy
  slightly cloudy (blurry)
  cloudy
  turbid
  dirty
  milky
+ muddy

LEVELS OF BRIGHTNESS IN WINE

- crystal clear
  brilliant
  bright
  dull
+ dim

HOW TO EXAMINE WINE VISUALLY

All the visual elements of a wine, whether it is white, red or rosé, should be appreciated in the following way:

Hold the glass by its base, between the thumb and forefinger, in order to avoid obstructing the color of the wine with your hand (and also to avoid heating up the wine). Bring the glass to eye level, with a source of light in front of you, so that you may observe the hue and the intensity of the color by the light that shines through it. Then examine the wine from above, putting the glass on a white prop and tilting it slightly so that the surface of the wine — known as the *disk* — becomes oval-shaped. Thus you may observe the reflections, the clarity and the brightness of the wine. Gently tilt the glass to bring the wine close to the rim, then tilt it back to vertical position: long droplets, known as "tears" or "legs", can be seen on the side of the glass. Their quantity, thickness and speed as they slide down the side of the glass tell us about the alcohol level, viscosity and overall richness of the wine.

With regards to sparkling wines, the quality of the bubbles may be appreciated:
– Through the persistence of the foam after the wine has been poured into the glass,
– Through the number and size of bubbles,
– Through the formation (or absence) of thin, continuous (or discontinuous) strings of bubbles and of a crown of bubbles on the surface.

HOW WE SMELL

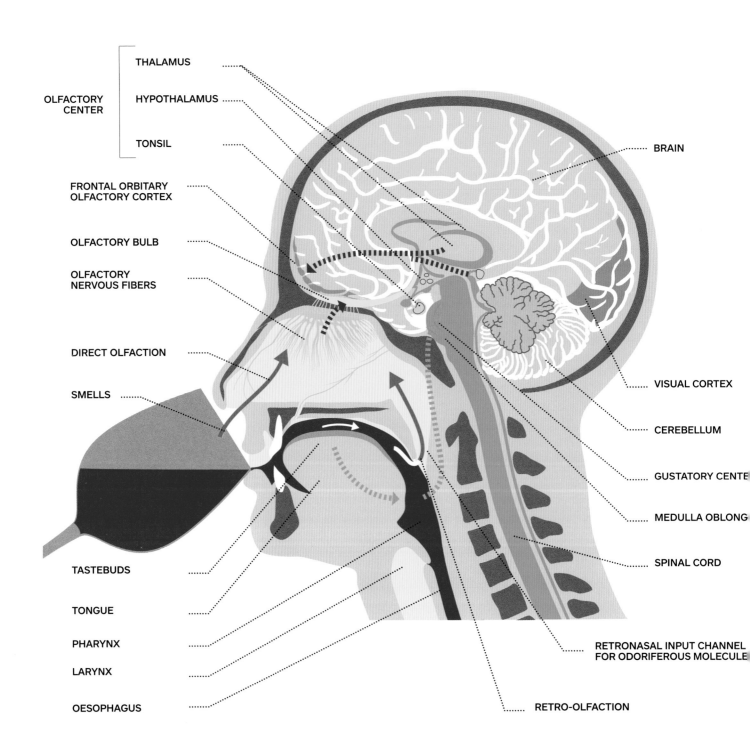

THALAMUS

HYPOTHALAMUS

TONSIL

OLFACTORY CENTER

FRONTAL ORBITARY OLFACTORY CORTEX

OLFACTORY BULB

OLFACTORY NERVOUS FIBERS

DIRECT OLFACTION

SMELLS

TASTEBUDS

TONGUE

PHARYNX

LARYNX

OESOPHAGUS

BRAIN

VISUAL CORTEX

CEREBELLUM

GUSTATORY CENTE

MEDULLA OBLONG

SPINAL CORD

RETRONASAL INPUT CHANNEL FOR ODORIFEROUS MOLECULE

RETRO-OLFACTION

THE ORGANOLEPTIC CHARACTERISTICS OF BORDEAUX WINE VARIETIES

REDS

Cabernet sauvignon: elegance and structure. Black fruit: blackcurrant, blackberry, spices, plum, bell pepper. Animal aromas, freshness, acidity, a beautiful tannic structure.

Merlot: red and black fruit (cherry, blackberry), violet. Animal aromas, licorice, truffle (depending on the terroir). Toasted notes; a full fleshy, velvety attack, complementing the tannic structure of cabernet sauvignon in blends.

Cabernet franc: red fruit (raspberry, cherry). Floral, spicy notes, a fine tannic structure but the tannins are smooth. Bright aromas, acidity and freshness.

Petit verdot: intense black fruit notes (blackberry, blackcurrant, blueberry), as well as violet, iris, menthol and licorice. Dense and solid.

WHITES

Sémillon: richness, finesse, delicateness, smoothness, deliciousness. Notes of almond, hazelnut, fresh butter, pear, acacia blossom, mango, candied apricot, peach. As a *liquoreux* (sweet) wine: notes of candied citrus, honey, toasted nuts (almond, hazelnut). A smooth, round and opulent mouthfeel. Naturally complements sauvignon.

Sauvignon: freshness, an acidity that does not prevent smoothness, liveliness, complexity. This grape variety is rich in volatile thiols (aromatic components producing olfactory notes of box tree or gorse). Powerful citrus notes (lemon, grapefruit or citron peel), blackcurrant bud, white peach, pear, white flowers. Warm smoky notes (flint, gunpowder).

Muscadelle: powerful, musky aromas. Round, low in acidity. Aromas of orange and mandarin zest, honeysuckle, acacia blossom, moscatel.

SECOND STAGE: THE NOSE

The olfactory examination is the second stage of a tasting. It aims to determine the different aromas that may be found in a wine, and to define their intensity — weak, medium, strong, pronounced… — and their quality — straightforward, elegant, delicate, open, youthful, expressive…

TWO DIFFERENT WAYS OF SMELLING

The nose is the organ of olfaction. Aroma-laden air enters through the nostrils before being carried and concentrated at the bottom of the nasal cavity where an extremely sensitive lining, known as olfactory mucous membrane, is found. That membrane is dotted with olfactory cilia — direct extensions of neurons connected to the olfactory bulb, which is the part of the brain located just above it. Odor-bearing molecules dissolve in the olfactory mucous membrane and act on the olfactory cilia, which transmit the information to the olfactory bulb via brain cells. The brain detects and analyzes this information and in turn, provided it recognizes it, triggers certain body functions. The more volatile and highly concentrated the flavor is, the more olfactory cilia will be stimulated and the stronger and clearer the olfactory perception analyzed by the brain will be.

There are two possible ways for smell to reach the olfactory mucous membrane:

• The direct nasal path (breathing in through the nostrils): the perception of aroma directly depends on how much of the odoriferous molecule is present in the air, and on how strongly we breathe it in.

• The retronasal path, i.e. sensing odors when we breathe out in the internal passage between the mouth to the nasal cavity. The warming-up of the wine in our mouth, the way it is spread around the mouth by tongue and cheek movements, and the slight internal pressure exerted by movements of the pharynx when swallowing, have the combined effect of slightly increasing the release of aromas. Therefore, the retronasal path generally gives more effective and decisive results than the nasal path.

THE ELEVEN AROMATIC FAMILIES

The eleven aromatic families are:
Animal – balsamic – woody – chemical – spicy (including some other aromatics than spices properly speaking) – empyreumatic – ethers (including some fermented aromas) – floral – fruity – mineral – herbaceous.
Here are the types of aromas defined by these eleven families:

ANIMAL
Game, venison, game stew, leather, fur, wild animal, Havana cigar...

BALSAMIC
Pine tree, pine nut, resin, resinous trees...

WOODY
Oakwood, wood, green wood, dry wood, damp wood, pencil, cedarwood, cigar box, mild tobacco...

CHEMICAL
Alcohol, menthol, vinous aroma, iodine, brine, controlled oxidation, madeirized (rancio)...

SPICY
Dill, aniseed, star anise, fennel, cinnamon, ginger, juniper berry, clove, nutmeg, black pepper, green peppercorns, pink peppercorns, basil, spearmint, peppermint, thyme, rosemary, oregano, bay leaf, garlic, licorice, vanilla bean, strong tobacco, truffle, girolle mushroom, cèpe mushroom (porcini), morel mushroom...

EMPYREUMATIC
Smoke, smoked foods, cooking smells, grilled, toast, caramel, frankincense, burned stone, flint, gunpowder, wood coal, roasted coffee, cocoa...

ETHERS
Green apple, green banana, fruit drops...

FLORAL
Acacia blossom, orange blossom, hawthorn, wild rose, tulip, honeysuckle, magnolia, hyacinth, lemongrass, heather, peony, rose, iris, violet, carnation, gentian, gorse, chamomile, lime blossom, lemon verbena, honey, beeswax...

FRUITY
Fresh grapes, grape jam, dried currants, moscatel, sour cherry, red cherry, kirsch, cherry stone, plum, prune, stewed fruit, quince, apricot, peach skin, peach stone, pippin, golden delicious apple, pear, dried fruits, almond, walnut, hazelnut, pistachio, wild berries, bilberries, blackcurrant, blueberries, blackberry, redcurrant, gooseberry, raspberry, strawberry, wild strawberry, melon, bergamot, lemon, orange, grapefruit, pineapple, ripe banana, date, passion fruit, mango, papaya, lychee, fresh fig, dried fig, honey...

MINERAL
Flint, quartz, schist, limestone...

HERBACEOUS
Grass, hay, vine leaf, vine stem, vine gimlet, green bell pepper, red bell pepper, crumpled blackcurrant leaf, dried leaf, fern, verbena, lime, tea, tobacco leaf, box tree, unripe fruit, green bean, fresh pea, asparagus, artichoke...

AROMAS

Most substances have smells. An aroma is a volatile chemical molecule that is carried by the air and perceived through our nose.

There are three categories of aromas in wine:
• Primary aromas: these are the aromas of the various grape varieties that are the basic components of wine.
• Secondary aromas: these occur in the wine during the various stages of fermentation.
• Tertiary aromas: these appear in the wine during its aging in barrel or in bottle. They may be due to the type of container — the oak barrel for instance — or be the result of the evolution of primary aromas over a period of time.
All these aromas dissolve into the wine, forming a complex composition that slowly homogenizes and harmonizes in the bottle until it becomes what is known as the *bouquet*.

AROMATIC FAMILIES

Aromas may be classified into eleven aromatic families (see page 140). Some are generally considered pleasant, others less so, but technically the limit between pleasant and unpleasant is often blurry; here is why:

– One given aroma that is present in small quantities in a certain type of wine may be perceived as a quality, but it may also become a flaw if it is more concentrated or present in another type of wine where it is not usually found.

– It is also a personal option as to whether an aroma is pleasant of not.

HOW TO SMELL WINE

The bouquet, as expressed by the most aromatic components, depends on the serving temperature and on how the wine is aerated. Thus, the olfactive examination is performed in two stages, both of which rely on the glass being held in a specific way.

• First nose

Gradually bring the glass closer to your nose, taking care not to agitate the wine, and begin smelling the wine with the glass is at a distance of about 4 inches from your nose, then half-inch by half-inch, ending up right above the rim of the glass. This first test allows us to define the intensity and quality of the wine's smell, and to discover its most prominent aromas.

• Second nose

Swirl the wine in the glass to aerate it, then smell the wine again. This process has the effect of intensifying the aromas perceived at the first nose stage and revealing other less intense aromas. The test may be taken further by gently smelling the wine while keeping the mouth open: other aromas are then revealed.

HOW TO SWIRL WINE IN THE GLASS

Beginners are usually intimidated by this gesture, but it is actually quite easy to master. Start practicing on a flat surface covered with a cloth (a tablecloth is perfect). Holding the base of the glass firmly with your fingers on top, start rotating it clockwise, slowly at first then a little faster. This rotation on a horizontal axis causes the liquid to rotate regularly against the sides of the glass. The movement should not be stiff but smooth, and the speed gradually increased. As you master this gesture, you will be able to repeat it without a prop, firmly holding the foot and stem of the glass and ensuring its rotation axis remains horizontal.

THAT DREADED CORK TAINT

In spite of every effort made by winemakers and by those who handle, carry and sell the wine, sometimes a bottle will show some aroma faults that alter its quality, prevent the expression of its terroir, or even make drinking it impossible. These faults may be related to smell and to the evolution of wine, or they may have to do with the way the wine was made, transported, or stocked. The most frequent problem — although it is now becoming rarer — is a corked aroma, or cork taint. Dreaded by both wine lovers and professionals, this defect (about which there are lots of misunderstandings) has a known point of origin, but it is difficult for a winemaker to prevent it. The smell is caused by a molecule (TCA) in the environment, and only minute quantities are required for the corked smell to be perceptible. The main carrier is natural cork, which could be responsible for up to 95% of cases. Aware of that problem, winemakers try to avoid its occurrence by using less risky types of closure (agglomerated cork, synthetic materials, screw-top caps that preserve the freshness of white wines, etc.), by checking the corks before bottling, by monitoring the atmosphere of their cellars on a regular basis, or by using metal or plastic pallets.

THIRD STAGE: IN THE MOUTH

Before moving on to the gustatory examination of the wine, it may be useful to reflect on the scientific definition of taste. Gustatory perception is the result of the combination of various sapid substances, categorized into four basic tastes:

• Sweetness is defined by a pleasurable, sugary, mellow sensation. In the case of wine, the term "mellow" or *moelleux* is more generally used, because the way we perceive it has more to do with unctuousness, smoothness and richness than with sugar *per se*.

• Saltiness is defined by a slightly biting and acrid character, without a notable change in the amount of saliva. This sensation is relatively seldom encountered in wine.

• Acidity is defined by a biting or sharp character, while the sides of the tongue seem to tighten towards its center.

• Bitterness is defined by an unpleasant, harsh and persistent sensation, along with a decrease in salivation and a dry sensation in the mouth. It is quite rare to find this in quality wines.

To these four basic tastes, we need to add the sense of lingual and palatal touch, which allows us to perceive the following sensory stimulations:

• Mechanical (rough, astringent, dry, structured, thick, velvety, silky…). Generally these are a result of the tannins.

• Thermic (warm, cold), depending on the temperature at which the wine is served.

• Chemical (the bite of carbon dioxide; the burn of alcohol…).

HOW THE TONGUE WORKS

The tongue is the main organ of taste. Its surface is composed of small captors known as taste buds. Each one of these taste buds has a shape, a particular spatial configuration that makes it more receptive to some strong-tasting substances than to others. When a sapid substance — sweet, acidic… — attaches itself to the taste bud that has an affinity with it, it activates a stimulus that conveys the information to the nervous system through an electrical impulse.

THE BALANCE OF A RED WINE

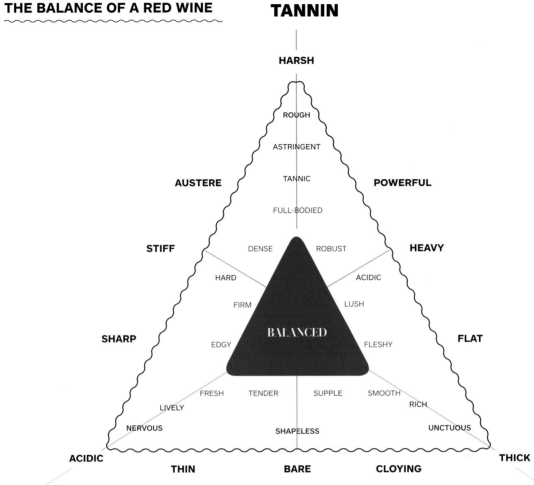

TANNIN

HARSH

ROUGH

ASTRINGENT

TANNIC

FULL-BODIED

AUSTERE   POWERFUL

STIFF   DENSE   ROBUST   HEAVY

HARD   ACIDIC

FIRM   LUSH

SHARP   BALANCED   FLAT

EDGY   FLESHY

FRESH   TENDER   SUPPLE   SMOOTH

LIVELY   RICH

NERVOUS   SHAPELESS   UNCTUOUS

ACIDIC   THICK

THIN   BARE   CLOYING

ACIDITY   **SWEETNESS**

The brain detects and analyzes that information and, if it recognizes it, triggers certain body functions in return, such as reactions of the nervous system, or salivation.

The more concentrated a sapid substance is, the more stimuli are triggered, thus increasing the number of electrical impulses transmitted to the brain, which then, in return, cause the body functions to react at a level directly proportionate to the intensity of flavor of the sapid substance.

THE TECHNIQUE OF GUSTATORY ANALYSIS

Analyzing the wine in the mouth is a rather complex process, which may be described as follows:

• Take a little wine in your mouth and chew it. Move it all around, coating the inside of your mouth, so that it stimulates all the taste buds. This allows us to experience the various gustatory perceptions and to evaluate the overall balance of the wine.

THE BALANCE OF A WHITE WINE

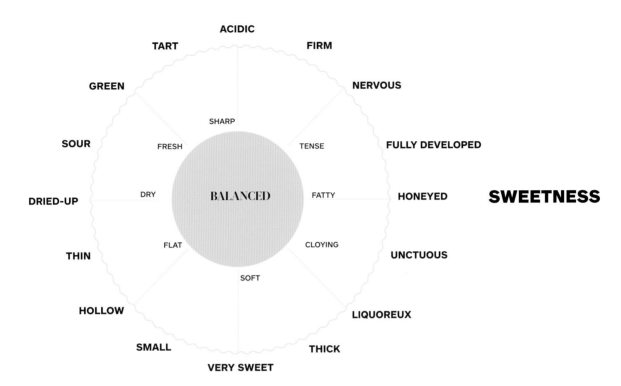

ACIDITY

SWEETNESS

(diagram labels, outer ring clockwise from top:) ACIDIC · FIRM · NERVOUS · FULLY DEVELOPED · HONEYED · UNCTUOUS · LIQUOREUX · THICK · VERY SWEET · SMALL · HOLLOW · THIN · DRIED-UP · SOUR · GREEN · TART

(inner ring:) SHARP · TENSE · FRESH · FATTY · DRY · BALANCED · CLOYING · FLAT · SOFT

• While chewing the wine, breathe in a little air through your mouth, then expel it through your nose. The air will exhale the wine's aromas, including the ones that are less intense. Once the air has been expelled, you will be able to identify more aromas which will inform your tasting of the wine. This technique is known as retro-olfaction.

• Spit out the wine, and measure the amount of time during which the aromas remain present in your mouth without any decrease in intensity. This short period of time can be measured in seconds — known in French as *caudalies* — and determines the length of the wine. At the same time, pay attention to the quality of the finish (the final sensation in the back of the mouth): it is important that the wine ends on a positive note, for the last impression is the one that leaves the deepest mark.

SITTING
DOWN **TO EAT**

Now comes the crucial part. The bottle, after waiting patiently in the darkness of the cellar, has arrived on the table. This is precisely where the accomplishment of wine, its very reason for being, is revealed for one should never forget that the destiny of wine is primarily to be paired with food and highlight its flavors. And it would be a shame to spoil such a lovely moment with mistakes that could ruin the small treasure sitting in that bottle. Here are a few precautions that are worth knowing.

0.375 L
HALF-BOTTLE

0.75 L
1 BOTTLE

1.5 L
2 BOTTLES

3 L
4 BOTTLES

5 L
6.66 BOTTLES

6 L
8 BOTTLES

12 L
16 BOTTLES

15 L
20 BOTTLES

18 L
24 BOTTLES

HALF-BOTTLE

BOTTLE

MAGNUM

DOUBLE MAGNUM

JEROBOAM

IMPERIAL

BALTHAZAR

NABUCHODONOSOR

MELCHIOR

UNCORKING THE RIGHT WAY

This is an important detail: the wine should never come in contact with the metal cap that protects the cork; it is therefore necessary to cut that cap below the ring (the bulging part at the top of the bottle). This is done by cutting the metal around the neck with the blade of a non-serrated knife, without rotating the bottle. If the neck is covered with sealing wax, break the wax gently by hitting it in several places, or better: try to remove it from the top of the neck with a knife, while avoiding shaking the bottle or the wine.

Speaking of tools, a "waiter's friend" or "sommelier" corkscrew is the best type to use. Introduce the screw into the center of the cork, taking care not to break it; place the tip of the lever on the lip of the bottle, then pull the arm gently upwards. The bottle should not move at all during the entire operation. Once the cork is out of the bottle, carefully wipe dry the lip of the neck with a clean cloth.

PAY ATTENTION TO TEMPERATURE

The expression of the aromatic components of a wine's bouquet depends on how volatile they are; and this is conditioned by the serving temperature. Indeed…

• If the wine is served too cold, it will not express any bouquet, or very little.

• If the wine is served too warm, oxidation can happen, or the destruction or unwanted combination of extremely volatile aromas can occur, as also can the emission of heavy aromatic elements. These can also be perceived on the palate, when combined with the unpleasant sensation of thermal shock. The serving temperature depends on the color of wine, on its age, on its organoleptic qualities and on the type of food it is to be paired with. However, for all wine, it is important to bring it slowly to serving temperature and to avoid heating it up too quickly. Finally, do not forget that a wine warms up quickly once it has been poured into the glass, and soon reaches room temperature (gaining 4 to 5 degrees in five to ten minutes).

15 - 18 °C
59-65 °F
RED WINES

9 - 10 °C
48-50 °F
MOELLEUX
(SEMI-SWEET)
AND LIQUOREUX
(SWEET) WINES

11 - 12 °C
52 - 54 °F
DRY WHITE WINES

8 - 10 °C
47-50 °F
ROSÉ, CLAIRETS
AND SPARKLING WINES

THE RIGHT TEMPERATURE

This is much more than a point of detail: the serving temperature dramatically influences the organoleptic qualities of the Bordeaux wine you are about to serve. Here are a few points of reference:
A young dry white wine, a sparkling wine or a clairet will be at its best between 45 and 52 °F (7 to 11 °C).
A structured, rich dry white wine or a liquoreux will be best served between 48 and 54 °F (9 to 12 °C).
Young, fruity red wines will be better tasted, depending on the season, from 57 to 61 °F (14 to 16 °C) — they are indeed drunk at cooler temperatures in Summer.
Finally, a great, aged red Bordeaux will express the best of its aromas between 61 and 65 °F (16-18 °C). Pay attention to the time of year — in Summer, a wine may warm up by several degrees in just a few minutes.

CARAFE OR DECANTER?

We know that wine needs oxygen to express its aromas; but oxygen can either be wine's best friend or its worst enemy. Once opened, a bottle evolves in contact with oxygen. Chronologically speaking, it goes from the "closed" stage to the "aerated" stage, before reaching the "oxidized" stage.

The time that separates these three successive stages depends on the age and structure of the wine. The wine reaches its taste peak at the aerated stage, and then moves more or less quickly towards the oxidized stage, which tastes unpleasant.

Young wines need more oxygen than the more fragile aged wines, which should not be submitted to any kind of shock or to excess contact with air. Therefore, young wines and aged wines need containers of different shapes. The carafe, designed for young wines, has a wider, flatter shape, offering wine a larger air contact surface for better aeration, which intensifies the aromatic expression — whereas the decanter, designed for aged wines, is narrower, offering a reduced surface for a more delicate aeration.

CARAFING, FOR YOUNG WINES

Carafing, or pouring a wine in a carafe, is a technique applied to young wines — as a rule, those less than seven years old. A young red wine tasted right after the bottle has been opened tends to display an overly assertive, sometimes unpleasant level of tannin, and insufficiently expressive aromas: the wine is then described as "closed". Pouring such wines into a carafe produces a contact with oxygen and allows their full expression, releasing aromas and rendering tannins softer and silkier, which in turn results in a better enjoyment of the wine.

Aeration intensifies the aromatic expression; thus a young wine should be aerated to display the full range of its complexity. Contrary to common belief, carafing is not only for red wines. Some very fine white wines with racy acidity, like Pessac-Léognan or Sauternes, deserve some aerating too.

One tricky question remains: how long should a wine be aerated for? Actually, there is no practical rule, each wine being different from one bottle to another. Generally, the more tannic a wine is, the longer the carafing time it requires before it can release its most delicate aromas. An aeration of 30 to 45 minutes is generally enough to appreciate the delicateness and complexity of a wine.

CARAFE, FOR YOUNG WINES

DECANTING, FOR AGED WINES

Decanting is based on an entirely different rationale: it is meant to eliminate various types of sediment that condense at the bottom of a bottle over time. This sediment varies in shape and density depending on the type of wine, on its quality and on the vintage. It may be composed of tartar precipitates (which look like crystals) or of color pigments (which look either muddy or light and fine-grained), or of a combination of both. Some types of sediment stick to the sides of the bottle, others stay suspended in the wine at the slightest movement of the bottle. Whatever type they are, they should not be considered abnormal, far from it — they are a natural testimony of the passage of time of the wine in a bottle. Thus, before serving a wine that contains sediment, it should be separated by delicately pouring the wine into a decanter. However, during such a transfer, the wine undergoes a lot of aeration — and thus oxidation. An aged bottle is a wonderful but fragile balance that may be destroyed in a few seconds if air comes into violent contact with the wine. Decanting should then be done as gently as possible to respect the integrity of wine. Finally, do not forget that, before any decanting, you should always taste the wine to check whether or not it can withstand such an operation.

HOW TO DECANT A WINE

Before decanting, the bottle should be left standing upright for one hour at room temperature. Traditional protocol recommends that it should be put in a bottle holder (which helps in handling the bottle and pouring out its contents more gently), but this is in no way compulsory. Uncork the bottle without moving it. Rinse the decanter with a few drops of wine from the bottle, then pour this small quantity of wine in a glass and taste it. Light a candle (this is another entirely optional element of protocol — any source of light will do). Proceed to the transfer by holding the decanter in one hand and the bottle holder (or the bottle) in the other hand, and gently pour the wine, which should slide down the sides of the decanter. At the end of the process, position the shoulder of the bottle above the source of light so that you may see the sediment through the glass as soon as it appears. Once the sediment starts to slide down the neck of the bottle, lift the bottle quickly to prevent it from falling into the decanter. The wine should then be drunk within an hour.

DECANTER, FOR AGED WINES

AN INFINITE NUMBER OF
PAIRINGS

Needless to say, all the style and finesse of Bordeaux wines are best expressed around a dinner table. But which wine should you serve with which dish? Certainly, some key principles should be respected, but do not forget that this choice also depends on taste, passion, or inspiration, and should be made according to personal choice or the mood of the moment. Thus there are classic pairings as well as "discovery" pairings, associating wines with unusual dishes or with different world cuisines.

With a young, fruity, tangy, fresh, even acidic dry white wine, it is worth trying, for instance, to recreate the atmosphere of a Spring morning. The wine may be paired with a crunchy mixed greens salad, with a lightly vinegared dressing (or perhaps seasoned with lemon juice) and enriched with lightly sautéed prawns; it may also be paired with oysters, raw marinated wild salmon, or a fillet of line-caught sea bass baked in parchment paper. Also remember that it is excellent served as an aperitif and that it may also lighten a cheese or dessert course, with fresh goat cheeses, fresh fruit or citrus sorbet for example. This type of wine also goes very well with Japanese food and raw fish dishes in general.

A rich and fruity dry white wine, fuller-bodied with a longer finish, possibly fermented or aged in oak barrels, will summon up ideas of lavish Mediterranean feasts and strongly flavored vegetable dishes, or fish, or white meats.

BORDEAUX WINES AND FINE DINING

There is more than one way to pair Bordeaux wines with food. While, historically, good wines have always accompanied good meals, favoring a harmony that increases pleasure and intensifies the feeling of communion around a table, their role is not limited to that. A glass sipped in the evening after returning home from work is a genuine moment of relaxation and enjoyment. The *apéritif* — the pre-meal drink — is another special moment. Its more modern equivalent, the aperitif served with food, extends and amplifies this trend by reaffirming that ageless love story between wine and gastronomy: the main purpose of a wine is to harmonize its qualities to the qualities of food. Actually, the best food-friendly wines are the ones that were made respecting the terroir. They are the wines that lend themselves to the most impressive pairings. Through their balance and diversity of flavor, Bordeaux wines are the most perfect companions for good food. Their worldwide success should not lead us to overlook that first and foremost, their purpose is to bring pleasure to a meal, especially considering that they have a precious, rarely mentioned special quality, which is digestibility. In the 18th century, Médoc and particularly Pauillac wines were regarded as a form of medicine.

Both healthy and delicious, drunk in moderation, Bordeaux wines are the friends of human physiology. Delicious by themselves, they acquire an extra dimension when associated with a well-chosen dish. This epicurean dimension of Bordeaux wine should never be overlooked.

It can slip easily and gracefully from a dish of grilled red mullet with *girolles* wild mushrooms to a tuna tartare, but with its full flavor and ample structure it is also a worthy match with with guinea-fowl baked with apricots, a mixed vegetable tart, a zucchini and eggplant casserole, or a Bavarian cream pudding. If the blend includes a majority of sauvignon, you may safely pair it with any dish that includes black truffles (the wine has to be sufficiently aged) or with Chinese or Japanese dishes: steamed *dim sum* dumplings, sushi... It is also a very good match with Northern Thai and Laotian Isaan dishes like grilled marinated chicken, lemongrass sausage, cuttlefish and bean thread noodles salad with lime juice, coconut milk fish custard... And finally, it will taste wonderful with a platter of matured cheeses.

A raw, fruity brut sparkling white wine will give a festive feel to a shellfish or oyster platter, a few spoonfuls of caviar on special occasions, or a strawberry mousse.

A light, airy *moelleux* (semi-sweet) white wine will rejuvenate a classic dish of roasted duck with peaches, and embellish the flavors of a cow's milk blue cheese like fourme d'Ambert, or a thin-crusted pear tart.

In the category of discovery pairings, *moelleux* wines also accompany Thai food very nicely, as long as it is not overly spicy. They harmonize perfectly with Vietnamese food and various Indian cuisines, particularly Mughlai cuisine from North India (creamy, rich dishes with mild aromatic spices). Mexican cuisines, without excess chili, also belong to its repertoire of food pairings.

In the presence of a *liquoreux* white wine, with concentrated flavors and a long finish, some extravagance is allowed: pan-seared foie gras with fresh grapes, a fine game terrine, a chicken with truffles, an exceptional Roquefort or a delicious Stilton cheese, a moderately sweetened dessert. The range of exotic pairings for moelleux wines (Thailand, Vietnam, India) is the same for liquoreux wines, but the latter's special affinity with fiery hot Chinese cuisines (Sichuan, Yunnan, Hunan) and Indonesian or Malay foods should be noted.

A young, fruity, silky, light red wine summons up the atmosphere of a good bistrot or elegant brasserie meal, over a delicate roasted veal with morels, a veal kidney in mustard cream, a piece of Brie, and pears poached in red wine. This is a wine for family-style cooking and a great companion for all "bistronomique" styles of cuisines, which combine the refinement of haute gastronomy with a bistro atmosphere.

A more evolved red wine, with fruity and/or gamey aromas, silky tannins and a longer finish, will display all its charm on nice pieces of grilled or roasted beef — beef rib on the bone, fillet or ribeye steak, T-bone or porterhouse, or roasted prime rib. And, last but not least, on chocolate desserts.

An aged, powerful and full-bodied red wine, rich and generous with a very long finish, takes us into the realm of haute cuisine; but its talents also include turning a roasted leg of Pauillac lamb, a fillet of roe deer, a game pie or a cherry tart into exceptional dishes. This type of wine should also be tried with the incomparable taste of a first-quality aged *jamón ibérico de pata negra* — gamey, deep-flavored, buttery and slightly sweet.

Rosé or clairet wines work wonders on a Summer alfresco table or at a picnic lunch. Served cool, ideally in an ice bucket, they will be equally delicious with *plancha*-grilled squid, olive oil-marinated goat cheeses, all sorts of barbecued meats, or a mixed fish *parillada*. Also, do not forget about them when you are in the mood for Chinese food.

TAKING CARE OF WINE

*Wine is both powerful and fragile. While, in great vintages,
it is strong enough to withstand the test of time, any neglect in transport
and storage is likely to alter its quality. Here are a few tips to ensure
the welfare of your wines.*

A basic rule — that *wine is a living product* — should never be forgotten; therefore carrying and storing wine requires a few precautions, which are not difficult to implement.
First of all, transport is a high-risk moment for your precious bottles.

• Rule n°1: always carry your bottles upright to avoid spillage.

• Rule n°2: avoid carrying wines in exceedingly hot or cold weather. As a rule, avoid strong temperature contrasts that can disrupt the wine's qualities.

• Rule n°3: wine does not like being shaken. Before drinking a wine, a period of rest is recommended.

WHAT MAKES A GOOD CELLAR?

• The structure: the most suitable space is an underground cellar with a dirt floor, away from all vibration, with a small air vent facing north.
• The temperature should be constant throughout the year (about 54 to 57 °F, 12 to 14 °C). The cooler the cellar, the slower the wine ages. Wine ages more rapidly in a cellar where the temperature is too warm.
• The air humidity should also be constant throughout the year (about 70 to 80% of ambient humidity). Below that average rate, there is a risk of corks drying up, and above, there is a risk of mold attacking corks and bottle labels.
• The light should be subdued as much as possible, and fluorescent lighting should be avoided.

IF YOU DO NOT HAVE A CELLAR

You may want to invest in a wine chest or wine cabinet where your bottles will be stored at an ideal temperature. Or you may store your wine in a cool, dark place, as safe from temperature variations as possible. Store the bottles horizontally, spacing them far enough apart so that air can circulate easily.

HOW LONG CAN A WINE WAIT?

The life span of a wine depends:
• On the type of wine.
• On the vintage.
• On the appellation, and above all from the terroir where the wine was produced.
• On how the wine was made and aged.
• On the size of the bottle. In particular, you should be aware of the "magnum effect", whereby wines in that large-sized container (150 cl) age longer — for the amount of oxygen received through the cork is smaller in proportion to the overall mass than in a 75-cl bottle. This does require more patience from the owner, but generally this patience is well rewarded in time.
• On the storage conditions in the cellar.
In order to estimate as closely as possible how long a wine should age, all these parameters should be kept in mind, and above all the wine should be regularly tasted to check how it is evolving.

HOW TO READ A LABEL

MANDATORY INFORMATION

• Reference to the CIVB's interprofessional approval.

• The name of the AOC, followed by the mention "Appellation d'origine contrôlée".

• Identity of the bottler, with name, city, country, following the mandatory mention *"mis en bouteille par…"* (bottled by) or *"Embouteilleur…"* (bottler). For any bulk purchase that includes the name of the château: the name and address of the merchant (or brand name) and the name of the winemaker.

• TAV — *Titre alcoométrique acquis* or the percentage of alcohol, or alcoholic strength.

• Origin: indication of the member state of the European Union where the grapes were harvested and vinified, worded as "Produit de France" or "Produit en France", or any equivalent terms.

• Presence of possibly allergenic substances.

• Health warning message for pregnant women.

• Volume of wine contained in the bottle.

• Batch identification number.

READING A WINE LABEL

Not only can choosing a wine be a real challenge; deciphering the label can often be a source of mystery. Being able to understand the plethora of references may make all the difference when buying wine. Some information on a label is mandatory, and some is optional. Here is an outline of the two categories of information, to help you sort things out.

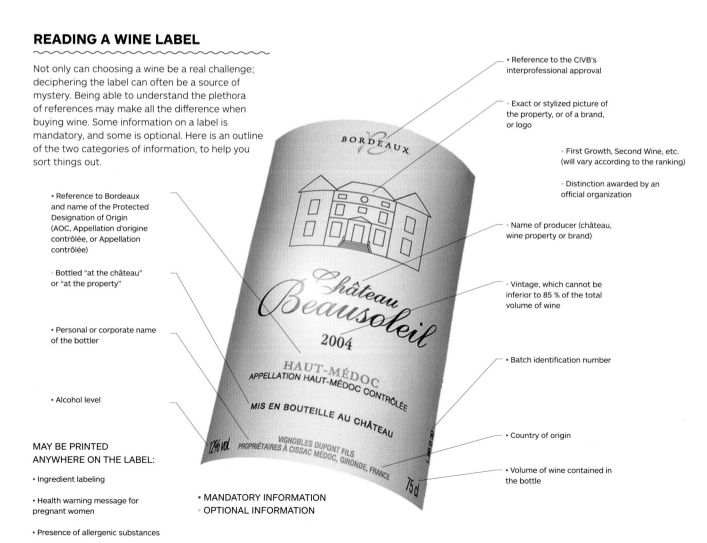

• Reference to Bordeaux and name of the Protected Designation of Origin (AOC, Appellation d'origine contrôlée, or Appellation contrôlée)

• Bottled "at the château" or "at the property"

• Personal or corporate name of the bottler

• Alcohol level

MAY BE PRINTED
ANYWHERE ON THE LABEL:

• Ingredient labeling

• Health warning message for pregnant women

• Presence of allergenic substances

• Reference to the CIVB's interprofessional approval

• Exact or stylized picture of the property, or of a brand, or logo

• First Growth, Second Wine, etc. (will vary according to the ranking)

• Distinction awarded by an official organization

• Name of producer (château, wine property or brand)

• Vintage, which cannot be inferior to 85 % of the total volume of wine

• Batch identification number

• Country of origin

• Volume of wine contained in the bottle

• MANDATORY INFORMATION
• OPTIONAL INFORMATION

HOW TO ESTIMATE THE OPTIMAL LIFE SPAN OF BORDEAUX WINES

WINE	CHARACTERISTICS	LONGEVITY
rosé and clairet		1 to 2 years, up to 3 years for a clairet
very dry white	young and fruity; a fresh, sharp balance; medium length	4 to 5 years
rich, fruity dry white	a round, ample, rich balance, with pronounced length. Can be vinified or aged in oak barrels	8 to 10 years, up to 15 to 20 years for great growths
sparkling white		4 years, sometimes 5
moelleux (semi-sweet) white	a light alcohol-sugar balance	8 to 10 years
liquoreux (sweet) white	a more pronounced alcohol-sugar balance, concentrated by the actions of noble rot	50 years and more
light, smooth red with low acidity	light in structure, a medium length	3 to 4 years
young, fruity red	a smooth balance, good acidity and moderately strong tannic framework, good length	5 to 8 years
older red wine	fruity and/or gamey aromas, a rich, full-bodied balance and a "melted" structure (silky tannins), very long finish	15 and up to 20 or 30 years for higher-quality wines
powerful red wine	fruity and/or gamey aromas, extremely long finish, well-structured	up to 30, even 50 years

OPTIONAL INFORMATION
• The wine estate. Year of harvest and/or name of the grape variety.
• Reference to a classification: *cru classé* (classified growth), *cru bourgeois…*
• The sugar content (mandatory for sparkling wines)
• Specific production methods — for instance "wine obtained from organically grown grapes", etc.
• Any metrological checks, meaning that the pre-packager certifies that the capacity of the containers conforms, and that it has been monitored accordingly.

WATCH THESE VIDEOS AND LEARN MORE

p. 8   p. 12   p. 16   p. 18

p. 23   p. 26   p. 28   p. 32

p. 34   p. 41   p. 42   p. 53

p. 54   p. 57   p. 59   p. 63

p. 67   p. 73   p. 77   p. 78

p. 79   p. 93   p. 100   p. 110

p. 113   p. 118   p. 119   p. 132

p. 133   p. 135   p. 139   p. 143

p. 147   p. 148   p. 151   p. 159

p. 160

AND ON THE INTERNET:

bordeaux.com
facebook.com/VinsdeBordeaux
twitter.com/VinsdeBordeaux
youtube.com/VinBordeaux
vimeo.com/vinsdebordeaux
flickr.com/photos/vinbordeaux
pinterest.com/vinsdebordeaux
instagram.com/vinsdebordeaux

Le vignoble de
de
BORDEAUX

Charente-Maritime

Charente

Dordogne

Lot-et-Garonne

Landes

OCÉAN ATLANTIQUE

GIRONDE

Appellations (map labels):

- Blaye
- Blaye Côtes de Bordeaux
- Côtes de Blaye
- Bourg
- Côtes de Bourg
- Fronsac
- Canon Fronsac
- Lalande-de-Pomerol
- Pomerol
- Lussac-Saint-Émilion
- Montagne-Saint-Émilion
- Saint-Georges Saint-Émilion
- Puisseguin-Saint-Émilion
- Saint-Émilion
- Saint-Émilion grand cru
- Francs Côtes de Bordeaux
- Castillon Côtes de Bordeaux
- Sainte-Foy-Bordeaux
- Graves de Vayres
- Entre-Deux-Mers
- Bordeaux Haut-Benauge
- Entre-Deux-Mers Haut-Benauge
- Cadillac Côtes de Bordeaux
- Premières Côtes de Bordeaux
- Cadillac
- Côtes de Bordeaux—Saint-Macaire
- Loupiac
- Sainte-Croix-du-Mont
- Médoc
- Saint-Estèphe
- Pauillac
- Saint-Julien
- Listrac-Médoc
- Moulis
- Margaux
- Haut-Médoc
- Pessac-Léognan
- Graves
- Graves Supérieures
- Cérons
- Barsac
- Sauternes

Towns: LESPARRE-MÉDOC, BLAYE, BORDEAUX, LIBOURNE, Castillon-la-Bataille, Sainte-Foy-la-Grande, LANGON, Bazas, Pellegrue, Monségur, Sauveterre-de-Guyenne, Créon, Targon, Podensac, Cadillac, La Réole, Grignols, Auros, St-Macaire, Pauillac, St-Laurent-Médoc, Mérignac, Pessac, Talence, Bègles, Gradignan, Villenave-d'Ornon, Le Bouscat, Floirac, Cenon, Lormont, Branne, Pujols, St-André-de-Cubzac, Bourg, Coutras, Guîtres, St-Savin

Pointe de Grave · La Verdon-sur-Mer · Soulac-sur-Mer

0   10 km

Legend:
- Rouge / Red / Rotwein / Rode wijn / 赤 / 红酒
- Rosé / Rosé / Roséwein / Roséwijn / ロゼ / 桃红酒
- Blanc sec / Dry white / Trockener Weißwein / Droge witte wijn / 辛口白 / 干白
- Blanc doux / Sweet white / Edelsüßer Weißwein / Zoete witte wijn / 半甘口白 / 甜白

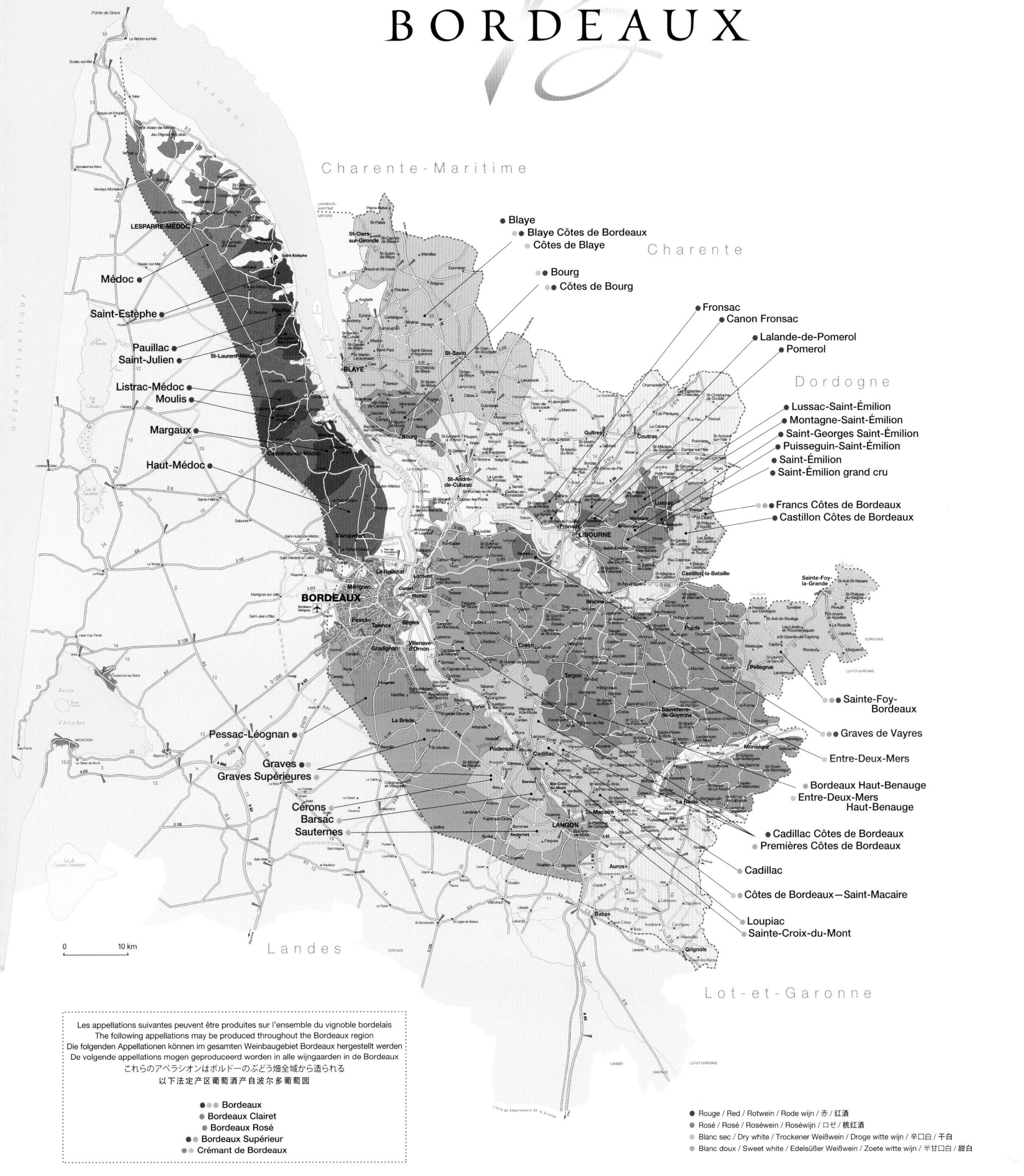

SOURCES

The economic data mentioned in this book refers to 2013, unless stated otherwise in text or captions.

PHOTOGRAPHY CREDITS

T = TOP, B = BOTTOM

© Mathieu Anglada, pages 6-7, 28, 128-129, 136, 156-157
© Gilles d'Auzac, page 42
© Vincent Bengold, page 68
© Alain Benoit, pages 29, 141, 152, 155
© Château La Dauphine, page 27
© CIVB, page 31 b
© Patrick Cronenberger, pages 22, 40, 45, 47, 60, 64, 70-71, 81, 82, 90 b, 91, 92, 104, 110, 113, 114, 121, 124, 135, 150, 162-163
© Christophe Goussard, pages 19, 89
© Musée des Douanes, page 30 t
© OTB – T. Sanson, page 20
© François Poincet, page 107
© Claude Prigent, pages 130, 153
© Philippe Roy, pages 10, 31 t, 36, 39, 43, 48-49, 51, 58, 90 t, 101, 116-117, 118, 125

Coordinating editor: Laure Lamendin
Original French text translated by Sophie Brissaud and edited by Datawords, Paris
Graphic design and layout: Grégory Bricout
Illustration: Mercè Cartañà

Distributed in 2015 by Stewart, Tabori & Chang
An imprint of ABRAMS

Copyright ©2014, Éditions de La Martinière, an imprint of EDLM.

Library of Congress Control Number: 2014956696

ISBN: 978-1-61769-164-5

Printed and bound in France
10 9 8 7 6 5 4 3 2 1

ABRAMS
THE ART OF BOOKS SINCE 1949
115 West 18th Street
New York, NY 10011
www.abramsbooks.com